CW00471343

Linda Hill

Highly Sensitive

Practical Strategies for Understanding Emotions,

Managing Relationships and Maximizing Your

Potential in an Overstimulating World

Linda Hill

Linda Hill

Table of Contents

Your Secret Gift #1

Get My Next Book

"Highly Sensitive - Part 2"

(Free for a limited time)

For a limited time, and as a "Thank you" for purchasing this book, you can be added to our "Book 2 Launch List" for free so you get the second book of this series when it gets published (This book will be priced at $24.99 and I guarantee it will be a great read). Simply visit the URL below and follow the instructions. You'll be the first to get it.

Visit here:

lindahillbooks.com/sensitive

Scan QR Code:

Your Secret Gift #2

Get the Audio Version for Free

If you would like to get the audio version of this book so you can read along or listen while you are in the car, walking around, or doing other things, you're in luck. For a limited time, I've provided a link that will allow you to download this audiobook for FREE. (This offer may be removed at any time).

Step 1: Go to the URL below.

Step 2: Sign up for the 30-day free-trial membership (You may cancel at any time after, no strings attached)

Step 3: Listen to the audiobook

Visit here:

lindahillbooks.com/sensitivepromo

Scan QR Code:

Introduction

In today's age in Western civilization, people are often put into categories: emotional or unemotional, warm or cold, thriving or miserable. Of course, when we observe things a bit closer, through a more nuanced lens, we realize that most of these issues are not black and white. Most traits exist on a spectrum, and empathy is no different. Some individuals are highly sensitive like emotional sponges, while others are lacking in empathy so much that they're actually considered psychopaths. And then there's the array of individuals who fall somewhere in the middle, making up the majority of the population. When you look at empathy this way, you can see why the highest level of sensitivity is actually incredibly rare. It's that rare percentage of people who make up the category of the highly sensitive.

Highly sensitive people (HSPs) are said to be as rare as psychopaths. They're the psychopath's opposite. Instead of being marked by a lack of feeling, they're characterized by their overwhelming heightened emotions. Scientists and psychologists alike now acknowledge the unique differences in our biological makeup. Some people were simply born with higher emotional levels, while others were born with other heightened mental capacities. Highly sensitive people are the kings and queens of sensitivity. Their brains were formed in such a way that they possess far more empathy than the majority of the people. Naturally, this kind of special advantage also contains within it several disadvantages. Even so, this extreme level of empathy is special, rare, and creates a highly unique experience that only true HSPs can understand.

Because highly sensitive people are so emotional, they possess a unique worldview which reflects that. These people tend to be reflective and shy, deep thinkers and natural poets. They feel everything on a grander scale and need lots of time to decompress from the overstimulation they're so prone to experiencing.

If you're reading this book, you may be curious about your own sensitivity. Maybe you can't help but sob at sad movies, or you find yourself feeling exceptionally anxious in high-pressure work situations. If this is the case, there is nothing wrong with you. You have a gift that deserves to be celebrated. Furthermore, you have powers that others don't have access to. Don't waste even a second wishing you were different. You have the capacity to live life in technicolor, with an abundance of love and a surplus of passion. And if you're wondering how to optimize these gifts and thrive as a highly sensitive person, you've come to the right place. Let this book serve as your guide and carry you forward with confidence, shining through your boundless empathy.

CHAPTER ONE

What Is a Highly Sensitive Person?

"They hear nearly every sound, notice every movement, and process the expression on every person's face. And that means that simply walking through a public space can be an assault on their senses."

— Andre Sólo, author at Introvert

Sensitive people are all around us, but highly sensitive people make up just a fraction of the population. When you consider just how intense and overwhelming the emotional life of a highly sensitive person is, their rarity and specialness begins to make sense. Highly sensitive people don't experience the world in the same way as everyone else. They notice things other people do not, they feel things on an infinitely deeper level, and they are all around more vulnerable to life's pain and cruelty. Think about the way an average person experiences emotions on a daily basis. Then, multiply that experience times five. That's the level of sensitivity highly sensitive people live with day to day.

For better or for worse, sensitive people don't get to choose their own sensitivity levels. They get no say in the matter; they're simply born that way. Further, many struggle to understand their power until they get older. For most people in modern society, sensitivity is seen as a weakness, but highly sensitive people actually have a gift. Their extreme vulnerability and general emotional natures allow them to see things others cannot. Highly sensitive people are always tuned-in to the emotional undercurrents of any given situation. They pick up on the subtlest of social cues without even trying. Therefore, they have a major upperhand in any and all social situations. They have the ability to understand how other people feel through an almost telepathic process. So, while their sensitivities present obvious challenges, they're also responsible for their greatest gift.

Signs of High Sensitivity

Before we address both the challenges and blessings of life as a highly sensitive person, it's good to understand what it means to be sensitive in general and what it means to be someone who is susceptible to emotional overload. Because no one person's experience is the same, there is a model known as the DOES model which outlines four basic characteristics of the highly sensitive person:

- Depth of processing

- Overstimulation

- Emotional responsiveness and empathy

- Sensitivity to subtleties

Depth of processing refers to the level in which any given person processes information. While many people process things on a shallow level, deep processing occurs when we process with more meaningful analysis. It's what occurs when we go deeper with a thought, exploring all its odds and ends.

Overstimulation is a defining trait for highly sensitive people. This refers to the HSP's sponge-like quality. They can't help but sense everything around them when they enter a new space. When you're overly sensitive toward your environment, you're going to be constantly at risk of overstimulation. It's as simple as that (Sensitive Evolution, 2012).

Emotional responsiveness and empathy are the third trademark of a highly sensitive individual. Typically, those who are highly sensitive are also highly empathetic. When you feel everything strongly on a personal level, you can also understand and relate to others who feel things strongly in their own personal way. Highly sensitive people have a special relationship to emotions. They tend to possess high levels of emotional intelligence and compassion. It's no wonder that highly sensitive people are also the best at feeling what other people are feeling. They're simply tuned into the emotional atmosphere around them.

Finally, highly sensitive people are marked by their sensitivities to subtleties. Most people who experience an average level of empathy don't live life tuned into the emotional undercurrents of every situation. They notice what's occurring on the surface but not necessarily what's below. Highly sensitive people, however, notice every facial expression, subtle mood, and slight shift in energy. They can absorb even the subtlest of emotional cues. If you're speaking to a highly sensitive individual, you don't have to state what you're feeling plainly in order for them to understand it. They'll pick up on your body language, subtext, and overall mood. The actual words you're saying are often less important than the way you deliver the information. Highly sensitive people are accounting for everything.

The sensory processing sensitivity trait can be considered a survival advantage in certain scenarios because it allows people to process information more thoroughly and boosts responsiveness to the environment and social stimuli (Philips, 2019). However, it also presents challenges. When you're absorbing so much intel from your environment, just the experience of daily life can become incredibly overwhelming. The most challenging part is that you can't turn it off. It would be great if HSPs could simply tell their brains, "Hey, can you chill out for just a second? I think I've reached my threshold." But, unfortunately, that is not how it works. Highly sensitive people walk around like sponges, noticing everything and drawing conclusions through deep thinking. This can be challenging when HSPs find themselves in tense situations. If they walk into a room where a group of people have just finished arguing, the HSP will feel that, and they may even wonder if the bad energy has something to do with them. These are the kinds of scenarios that are typical stressors for highly sensitive types. At the same time, though, no one is better equipped to revive a room with peace and harmony. It's this same quality that makes highly sensitive people amazing mediators and excellent listeners.

The best way to overcome emotional overload as a highly sensitive person is through practicing self-awareness and creating healthy boundaries. It can be incredibly taxing going through life feeling everything, wondering if you're the reason people are upset, and feeling guilty at the slightest awkwardness in human interactions. It's easy to ruminate on subtleties like these, but it's harmful to go down rabbit holes of negative thought. Therefore, you must establish boundaries with others to keep from absorbing other people's negative projections. We'll touch on that in future chapters. More importantly, though, HSPs need to set personal boundaries within the confines of their own brains to keep negative self-talk at a minimum.

Without these proper internal boundaries, HSPs can spiral and overthink to the point where there's nothing more to be gained. They can end up feeling inadequate, not because someone wanted them to feel that way but because through the process of overthinking, the HSP has simply come to that conclusion. You can see how this sort of habit is unproductive and harmful. The more self-aware HSPs are, the more they can catch themselves as this process is unfolding. If you're a highly sensitive person who spends too much time overanalyzing every situation, try to catch yourself before you enter the danger zone. A normal amount of analysis is healthy and good, but too much thinking can easily turn negative. Luckily, self-awareness comes naturally to highly sensitive people, so don't put yourself through more heartache than is necessary. Be kind to yourself and make your head a pleasant place to live. You'll be amazed at how the rest of your life falls into place.

The Science Behind Sensitivity

It's not that highly sensitive people are just more emotional for no reason. They actually have hyper sensitive mirror neurons in their brains—mirror neurons that are far more sensitive than the average person. While everyone has mirror neurons that allow them to experience empathy (with psychopaths being the exception), HSPs have overenergetic mirror neurons. This means that from the moment a highly sensitive individual is born, they are absorbing the emotional world around them like a sponge. Their brains are simply hardwired to soak up the mood of the atmosphere in which they inhabit. For the same reason, these people also have highly active intuitions and creative capacities. They experience life through a more nuanced lens, so they experience everything deeper and with more intensity.

If you're wondering if you may be a highly sensitive

person yourself, consider the situations that trigger your sensitivity. When your sensitivity is triggered, think about what that experience feels like. If a single harsh comment has the power to draw tears, for example, you may be a highly sensitive person. If you find that a sad movie elicits a reaction far more intense than that of your friends, you may also be a highly sensitive person. Or if you experience great emotional highs and lows, intense bouts of empathy, or lots of intuitive hunches, you're probably a highly sensitive person. Chances are that if you think you may be one, you probably are. Highly sensitive people know themselves better than most people.

Additionally, one of the trademarks of a highly sensitive individual is an extremely vivid inner life. This is part of the reason why empathic people know themselves so well—they spend a great amount of time in their heads. For highly sensitive people, the world is full of great meaning. The simplest moments may seem profound because HSPs refuse to live superficially. They can't help but search for the deeper meaning of things, and that requires a lot of internal musing and reflection. The inner world and imaginations of highly sensitive people are incredibly vibrant and colorful. They love to philosophize and think about abstract matters. They're also creatively gifted and motivated.

Challenges of High Sensitivity

About 15 to 20 percent of the population are said to be highly sensitive. Psychologists believe that it is a product of nature, but nurture plays a vital role as well. Most HSPs show signs of high sensitivity from as early as infancy. If you pay attention to the expressions and reactions of a highly sensitive infant, you'll notice how they're taking in the atmosphere through their deeply emotional lens. If their parents are unhappy, the baby will be unhappy. If the room is loud or the lights are too bright, the baby may have a negative emotional response. Even before they know how to speak or analyze, they're absorbing the emotional world around them and reacting based on those observations.

Then, as the highly sensitive infant grows older, they tend to experience a certain dynamic at home that either celebrates or complicates their sensitivities. For example, highly sensitive people are especially vulnerable to criticism. If they grow up in a household where criticism is dulled out consistently, they will feel extremely hurt and overwhelmed. HSPs can only handle so much criticism before they begin to internalize it. The worst is when highly sensitive individuals grow up in households where there is abuse or neglect. When this is the case, the HSPs often experience a major hit to their self-esteem. Most have to learn to separate their own emotions from that of others, but until they are able to do that, everything is blurry and confusing. If a parent or other family member tells them that they're no good, they will believe it rather than question that statement's legitimacy.

Highly sensitive people are so understanding of others, and so empathetic and compassionate, that they often neglect or repress their own feelings. This, of course, becomes a problem when HSPs find themselves around toxic people. It makes them especially vulnerable to abuse and mistreatment. It is all too easy for HSPs to forgive those who treat them poorly because they find it easy to see the beautiful potential in others. This is part of what makes highly sensitive people so special—they see the world and everyone within it through rose-colored glasses—but it's also the thing that has the potential to ruin their self-esteem and cause lots of mental and emotional damage.

Until HSPs have the ability to practice discretion, they're always vulnerable. Unfortunately, for most highly sensitive people, that vulnerability begins in childhood. It is all too common for HSPs to grow up in homes that lack the proper nurturance they require. Many HSPs grow up feeling misunderstood. At worst, they grow up walking on eggshells, which makes them deeply introverted but even better equipped to read a room and facilitate harmony.

If you're a highly sensitive person yourself, I hope that you grew up with a supportive family who celebrated your gifts and understood your sensitivities. If that's not the case, I hope you can find solace in the knowledge that your sensitivity and your past experiences make you strong. Tons of people wander through life never really feeling anything, but highly sensitive individuals are strong enough to embrace emotion knowing full well they will experience hurt. And that is the sign of a strong person (Sensitive Evolution, 2012).

Sensitivity as a Gift

Although life as a highly sensitive individual is certainly challenging, it also offers great beauty and depth. Beauty, in particular, is an HSP's special friend. Highly sensitive people have a special connection and relationship to beauty. They appreciate life and the objects within it, in more than just a superficial sense. They experience art, for example, differently than most people because they possess such a strong abstract lens. They pick up on more than just an image or a story, they also experience the feelings of the artist and the emotions surrounding the images. They experience art on an intuitive level; they don't just appreciate it intellectually but also through the eyes of the heart. Therefore, HSPs are more receptive to beauty in all forms. They can become overwhelmed by the view of a sunset or experience euphoria through a sweet sentiment from a friend. All these highs and lows present their fair share of challenges, but they also allow for a life that is rich with feeling and meaning. In many ways, highly sensitive people experience the world in a more profound way than the rest of the population.

As I've already mentioned, highly sensitive people are like emotional sponges. They absorb the energies around them with little say in the matter, and they must actively work to create boundaries if they wish to protect themselves from toxicity and mental burnout. Instead of existing as a separate person, removed from the rest of humanity, they experience life as if they are an intrinsic part of it. They feel how all of life is connected on an intuitive level. So, although they often feel misunderstood, taken advantage of, or overwhelmed, they also feel at home among the plants, animals, and the rest of humanity. They understand that we're all in this together. While their inner lives are vivid, and they tend to feel most comfortable alone in their heads, they always feel connected on a spiritual level to the beauty and profundity of life.

Chapter Summary

- Highly sensitive people feel everything on an infinitely deeper level.

- The four basic characteristics of the highly sensitive person are depth of processing, overstimulation, emotional responsiveness, and empathy.

- The best way to overcome emotional overload as a highly sensitive person is through practicing self-awareness and creating healthy boundaries.

- While everyone has mirror neurons that allow them to experience empathy (with psychopaths being the exception), HSPs have overenergetic mirror neurons.

- Highly sensitive people have a special connection and relationship to beauty. They appreciate life and the objects within it, in more than just a superficial sense.

In the next chapter, you will learn how to achieve a healthy lifestyle as a highly sensitive individual.

CHAPTER TWO

Health and Lifestyle of the HSP

"Highly sensitive people learned early in life to try to control the external world as a way to attempt to manage their inner one."
— **Sheryl Paul, Depth Psychology Counselor and author**

It's no wonder that all that sensitivity HSPs experience often leads to the sensation of feeling overwhelmed or depressed. When you're going through life as a vulnerable emotional sponge, you have the potential to feel overstimulated at any moment. So, what can highly sensitive people do to protect themselves and turn life into a more stable experience?

Unsurprisingly, self-care is especially important for highly sensitive types. In order for HSPs to stay happy and optimistic, they must make their mental health a top priority. Otherwise, it's all too easy to drown in the sorrows of negativity and allow life to spin out of control. But what does a healthy lifestyle look like for a highly sensitive individual? How can these people create routines that help them to thrive?

As mentioned in the previous chapter, HSPs are especially sensitive to their environments. They can easily become overwhelmed in crowded places that are full of big personalities. Even harsh lighting or loud noises have the potential to throw off an HSP and leave them feeling vulnerable and stressed. Combine this with the HSP's relationship to criticism, and you get someone who probably won't do well working 9 to 5 at a large corporate enterprise. Typically, highly sensitive people function better when they can work at home, with the comfort of their loved ones or pets. They need ample alone time to decompress and recharge before absorbing more energy out in the world. Ideally, HSPs should develop a lifestyle that allows for alone time and flexibility.

Value in Creativity

Highly sensitive people have the potential to become people-pleasers, so any job or lifestyle that puts too many demands on the HSP will likely have disastrous results. Highly sensitive people need to learn to put themselves first every once in a while, so a healthy lifestyle includes one where they can make their passions a priority. Many HSPs turn to a creative lifestyle for this reason; it allows them to embrace emotions all day while expressing themselves simultaneously. Through infusing their lives with creativity, they can celebrate their unique personalities in the comfort of solitude. Creativity can be a deeply healing experience for HSPs, so it's worth it to create room for it in their lives, even if they don't wish to pursue it professionally. Creativity allows HSPs to use their unique gifts to create something tangible. It combines their appreciation of nuance and beauty with their rich imaginations and emotional lens. It's quite rewarding for a highly sensitive person to take all of the beauty and deep observations which exist in their minds and turn them into something other people can appreciate. If you're a highly sensitive person yourself, consider making creativity part of your daily routine. You could choose to dabble with any of the following:

- Writing

- Journaling

- Dance

- Singing

- Music

- Drawing

- Painting

- Arts and Crafts

And there's dozens more! You may be shocked to see

how even a simple activity like journaling can prove effective toward cultivating a healthy and happy life.

Spiritual Practices

Daily spiritual practices may prove beneficial to highly sensitive people. HSPs consider the world to be a special and meaningful place. They can typically sense an underlying order to things through their highly-tuned intuitions. They can be especially receptive to synchronicities and profundity in all forms. So, it's no surprise that highly sensitive people tend to feel a special connection to spirituality. It's a comfort for HSPs to know that they are not alone, that even life's upsets provide helpful insights, and darkness exists so that light can exist as well. These sentiments give HSPs hope and motivation. Activities like daily meditation and prayer can serve as a huge comfort for HSPs. These activities help ground highly sensitive individuals and inspire them to continue spreading love to those around them.

However, it is quite difficult for highly sensitive people to find time for daily spiritual practices or daily opportunities for creativity when they are always at the mercy of other people's needs. In order for HSPs to find the alone time they need, they must learn to enforce proper boundaries. Without boundaries, HSPs may get into the habit of people-pleasing or entering codependent relationships where their needs are constantly put on the backburner. HSPs must use their empathy for good, but they must practice discretion when doing so. If they continually live for others while consistently abandoning themselves, they'll always suffer and they'll eventually find that they have no more empathy to give. Through making time for themselves and enforcing boundaries that protect them, HSPs can practice self-love and acknowledge their worth as individuals. When they take the time for themselves, they're telling their subconscious that they matter, too, which leads to happiness and more abundance in love.

Importance of Solitude

Alone time for highly sensitive people is incredibly important. HSPs need lots of recharge time because when they're out in the world, they're absorbing energy constantly. If they don't take time for themselves consistently and often, then it's only a matter of time before they break down at the grocery store or find themselves "overreacting" to something seemingly insignificant. All of the energy that they're constantly absorbing doesn't just evaporate. They have to let it out through solitude and self-care. By taking time for themselves and eliminating the outside energies when necessary, highly sensitive people can achieve inner peace. Once peace is established internally, they're ready to roam the world once more, embracing their feelings and absorbing life's energies all over again.

There are a number of reasons why highly sensitive people refuse the solitude they so desperately need. Codependency is one of those major reasons. When a couple is codependent, there's little room for alone time. The highly sensitive person would rather bend over backward for their partner, fulfilling every expectation and desire, than demand time to themselves. But the sooner HSPs take responsibility for their needs, the sooner they can thrive in a truly healthy lifestyle. Taking alone time requires the ability to say "no" every now and then. Generally, HSPs find it extremely difficult to say "no." They must realize that sticking up for themselves and advocating for their solitude will always make everyone happier. The only way to please others is to first please yourself. So, a healthy-sensitive lifestyle includes lots and lots of quality alone time.

Once HSPs do earn their alone time, they should work to embrace their emotions and accurately separate their feelings from that of others. Highly sensitive people are prone to taking on the emotions of others as if they are their own, so it's incredibly important that they take time to detach from their personal relationships. For example, let's say that a highly sensitive person has a friend who always wants to watch a specific television series. They're always inviting the HSP to join them, and since the HSP loves their friend, they join them almost every night. But then one day, the HSP can't make it. Perhaps they have an assignment due and don't have time for television that night. When they try to explain this to their friend, they respond by saying they understand, but it's evident that underneath that understanding, there is anger and disappointment. The highly sensitive person might blame themselves for disappointing their friend. They may feel like a bad friend, or even a bad person. But if they can detach and recharge, they can eventually learn to understand that these thoughts are far from the truth. The highly sensitive person is not responsible for other people's feelings. It's perfectly acceptable to ask for a night of solitude.

Setting Boundaries

In order to achieve a peaceful lifestyle, highly sensitive people must learn to separate themselves from others. They must make their own needs a priority and follow their passions. Otherwise, they will lose themselves in loved ones or in a society that doesn't celebrate their inherent worth. In the same vein, it's important that highly sensitive people build a life based on passion and authenticity rather than living by a parent or loved one's values. Because highly sensitive people feel everything so strongly, they need to do work that involves their heart and soul. They need to feel that their work and daily activities serve a higher purpose. HSPs should work hard to achieve the freedom and lifestyle they desire. If they live only according to the rules of others, they'll never find the happiness they so need. And, more than likely, they'll fall into bad habits.

Highly sensitive people are also far more likely to abuse substances than the average person. Usually, it is the most sensitive people who require escape routes from life's devastation. And there's no better escape than drugs and alcohol. According to Judith Homberg, author of the article "High Sensitivity as a Vulnerability Factor in Substance Abuse":

"Drugs are an escape, a way of coping with all the stuff going on in their heads. Just think of performers and artists. Highly sensitive people are often exceptionally creative, and in those circles you also see excessive use of addictive substances."

A relationship between high sensitivity and substance use has never really been scientifically proven, though there is a range of evidence that points to such a connection (Homberg, 2017).

HSPs should avoid getting lost in substances because they only diminish their light and purpose. Instead, highly sensitive people should strive to use their empathy as a superpower on a daily basis. They should offer help to those in need and use their unique worldviews to inspire those around them. They should let their love seep out of them, making the world a better place. When highly sensitive people are able to use their power in this way, they find fulfillment and an internal locus of peace which never dies or fades away.

Chapter Summary

- In order for HSPs to stay happy and optimistic, they must make their mental health a top priority.

- Highly sensitive people need to learn to put themselves first, so a healthy lifestyle includes one where they can make their passions a priority.

- Creativity can be a deeply healing experience for HSPs, so it's worth it to create room for it in their lives, even if they don't wish to pursue it professionally.

- Highly sensitive people can be especially receptive to synchronicities and profundity in all forms, so it's no surprise that they tend to feel a special connection to spirituality.

- Alone time for highly sensitive people is incredibly important. HSPs need lots of recharge time because when they're out in the world, they're absorbing energy constantly.

- HSPs should work hard to achieve the freedom and lifestyle they desire. If they live only according to the rules of others, they'll never find the happiness they need. This includes setting boundaries and maintaining appropriate relationships with drugs and alcohol.

In the next chapter, you will learn how to say "no" as a highly sensitive person and how to break people-pleasing habits.

CHAPTER THREE

People-Pleasing and Saying "No"

"High sensitivity is not a disease or a disorder. It's not something that needs to be overcome or fixed."

— Jenn Granneman, author at Introvert

For highly sensitive people, the necessity to please tends to be a major life theme. Since HSPs can feel what others are feeling so acutely, they often have a strong desire not only to help but to please. This is one of their many gifts that manifests as a double-edged sword. It's a gift because HSPs have a special ability to create pleasant surroundings. They can intuit how others are feeling and mold their own actions accordingly. However, this also comes with a hefty price to pay. Too much emphasis on people-pleasing easily leads to resentment, as well as an array of other negative emotions. So, highly sensitive people should learn when it's appropriate to accommodate for the sake of others and when it's necessary to say "no."

People-pleasing tendencies are often a product of a difficult upbringing. It's not so much a conscious choice as it is a habit developed from an unstable early home dynamic. When HSPs grow up in a home where they have to "be pleasant" for the sake of the family, people-pleasing becomes a natural way of life. It becomes a coping mechanism against feelings of inferiority and a learned way to avoid conflict. By anticipating the needs of those around them, HSPs can eliminate any possibility of confrontation or threats against harmony. For highly sensitive people, social harmony is everything. There are many common scenarios that highly sensitive children experience that ultimately lead to a people-pleasing coping mechanism. None of these scenarios put the HSP at fault. However, they are exceedingly illuminating in terms of understanding their psychological framework.

Dangers of People-Pleasing

Many HSPs grow up as the family scapegoat, meaning they are blamed for the unhappiness of the family members around them. Obviously, this is extremely traumatic for the young HSP. For example, it is all too common for highly sensitive children to act as the victim of a narcissistic parent's abuse. The highly sensitive child, through no fault of their own, may experience abuse in the form of yelling, bullying, or unfair blame just through the act of existing. When this occurs, the highly sensitive child learns how to walk on eggshells, doing everything they can to avoid emotional abuse. In the worst case, HSPs may internalize the blame and bullying, which inevitably destroys their self-esteem. The HSP learns that if they want to get along with others, they have to repress their own authentic feelings and make the feelings of others a priority instead. This may work for a while, but as the HSP grows older, they'll discover that their lack of authentic expression sabotages any opportunity for true connection.

Additionally, if an HSP is raised by a narcissistic parent, they may develop the belief that their feelings don't matter. Unlike highly sensitive people, narcissists struggle with empathy. They feel as though their feelings are all that matter, so there is no room for the emotions of anyone else. This is incredibly damaging for highly sensitive children. If they're used to narcissistic responses, they'll learn to bottle up their emotions, reject their feelings as unimportant, and negate their intuitions. They'll also develop the belief that they must always obey the wishes of others or otherwise suffer. With all that being said, people-pleasing is a common coping mechanism for children of narcissists.

Learning to Say "No"

At a certain point, HSPs who have grown into chronic people-pleasers must learn to say "no." But, of course, this is easier said than done. People-pleasing HSPs find it incredibly uncomfortable to put their own needs before those of others. That may sound like an advantageous and innocent quality, and it is to a certain extent. But it's impossible to live a happy life while abandoning your own needs and desires. This is one of the critical life lessons HSPs must learn.

Highly sensitive people crave authentic connections more than anything, but so long as they make pleasing a priority, they can never have the intimate connections they so desire. Authentic connections are born out of authentic self-expression. If HSPs continually say "yes" even when they want to say "no," they will eventually develop a great deal of resentment, and resentment is another feeling that stifles organic connection.

HSPs must learn to say "no," no matter how uncomfortable it may feel. They must learn to become self-aware in their people-pleasing tendencies so that they can acknowledge the urge to please as they are experiencing it. That way, they can ask themselves, in the moment, "Am I reacting this way to ensure harmony? Or am I reacting this way because it is a genuine reaction?" If they can accurately determine the source of their reactions, then they can practice self-honesty and can begin to act from a place of truth and self-love rather than coping mechanisms and fear.

Baby Steps

Every time an HSP exercises their right to say "no," they are telling themselves that they care about themselves. They're telling themselves that they deserve to be a priority and that they have every right to personal happiness. It's like an inner vow and acknowledgment that the HSP is their own protector. Although the HSP's friends and loved ones may react poorly to rejection or negation at first, they will eventually learn that the highly sensitive individual is someone who is worthy of respect. They will eventually give the HSP the freedom and space they so desperately need. With that respect, comes the opportunity for a more genuine connection, built on truth and authenticity.

But it's impossible to jump from being a people-pleaser

to living in one's truth all at once. It takes time, patience, and self-compassion to exercise saying "no" when it's incredibly foreign to your nature and upbringing. For this reason, highly sensitive people should start with baby steps. They shouldn't be too hard on themselves when they struggle with altering their people-pleasing habits.

If you're an HSP, start by looking for small ways to live by your truth. For example, if you need to buy something at a store, and you can't find the item you're looking for, try asking a sales associate to help. If the associate then returns and states that they couldn't find the item you were looking for, ask them to check in the back. Don't be afraid to express your honest needs, and try doing so in small ways in the beginning if it's too challenging at first.

A common scenario is when a friend or loved one of an HSP wants to do a certain activity but the HSP would rather have the day or night to themself. The HSP's instinct will be to join the friend in whatever activity they want to do because they know it will make the friend happy. However, if it's not also something that will make the HSP happy, then the activity and time spent together is not rooted in authenticity. So long as that is the case, the HSP is doomed to sabotage any attempts at genuine connection and happiness.

There is nothing malicious about the HSP's people-pleasing proclivities. They genuinely want everyone around them to be happy and feel at peace. But with this desire comes the sensation that HSPs are actually responsible for the feelings and mental states of those around them. This can be very damaging to the HSP. No one person can be responsible for the emotions of others. It's always going to be a losing battle. The disappointment that ensues when the HSP fails at maintaining the emotional equilibrium of their atmosphere can feel gut-wrenching for the highly sensitive individual. This is why HSPs should avoid taking on that responsibility to begin with. Instead, they should understand that every person on this earth is only responsible for their *own* emotional well-being, not anyone else's. Once HSPs can integrate that philosophy into their internal value system, they can live much happier and healthier lives.

Experts suggest the implementation of four basic steps in order for highly sensitive people to avoid taking on the emotions of others. These steps include the following:

1. Evaluating your own needs

2. Using your preferred mode of communication

3. Maintaining boundaries over time

4. Holding responsibility only for yourself.

Evaluating Your Own Needs

For many HSPs, the first step may prove the most difficult. That is because it's often very challenging for highly sensitive people to articulate or even identify their needs. Most HSPs spend so much time focusing on the needs of others, that they lack any clarity when it comes to their own needs and feelings. They can become totally confused when evaluating what's theirs vs. what belongs to others by internalizing projections and getting lost in the habit of pleasing loved ones. Before HSPs can practice saying "no," they must first learn to identify their own wants and needs. Meditation is a useful means toward accomplishing this. So is journaling and giving voice to the HSP's vivid intuition through creative endeavors. With practice, highly sensitive people can become experts at identifying and acknowledging how they feel. Then, they can find the courage to speak up for their needs and desires.

Using Your Preferred Mode of Communication

Once HSPs know what their needs are, they must learn how to communicate them. This is also tricky business for highly sensitive people because most did not grow up in households where their emotions were given voice. If HSPs grew up with the belief that there is no space for their feelings and needs, then they will have a lot of trouble articulating those needs as adults. It is nevertheless important that HSPs learn how to communicate; otherwise, at one point or another, they will become depressed. Again, it's hard to become an expert communicator overnight, especially if HSPs have not been given the opportunity to communicate as children and adolescents.

If you're an HSP who wants to gain more confidence in this area, start small or figure out what method of communication works for you. Sometimes, it's helpful to journal or write your feelings down before articulating them. You may even consider communicating in written form by writing someone a letter or message. Additionally, you can start by practicing communication with those people in your life who understand your sensitive nature. Then, you can build up the courage to state your needs at work and with those who have less understanding personalities. It takes practice, but soon enough, you'll find that communicating your needs isn't as scary as it once may have seemed.

Maintaining Boundaries Over Time

After you practice effectively communicating your

needs, you must learn to stand by those needs through maintaining appropriate boundaries. Boundaries are extremely important for highly sensitive people. If you're an HSP, maintaining boundaries is one of the main ways to ensure that you are keeping your people-pleasing tendencies in check. By creating and maintaining boundaries, you are protecting yourself against those situations in which you feel you *have* to cater to the feelings of others.

It is all too easy for HSPs to abandon their own feelings when someone close to them is in need. But, if they set rules such as, "from 9 p. m. to midnight, I need total privacy and isolation," then they guarantee that their needs take priority.

This is also huge when it comes to bolstering self-esteem. As uncomfortable as it may feel at first, once an HSP learns to exercise boundaries, they gain confidence and a new sense of power. They learn that their feelings *do* matter as much as everyone else's, and those close to the HSP learn to respect their needs more. Boundaries make everyone's lives better, but for HSPs it takes some time and effort to get used to setting them. That's why they have to keep their end goal in mind and remember that anyone who chooses *not* to respect their boundaries is probably not a friend worth keeping.

Holding Responsibility Only for Yourself

After they put boundaries in place, HSPs can navigate emotional responsibility with more clarity. By implementing those boundaries, HSPs learn to take responsibility for their own emotions and therefore give others the opportunity to do the same. HSPs have a tendency to attract people who do not want to take responsibility for their own feelings. Rather than blame these people, HSPs should learn to separate what's theirs from others'.

For example, a highly sensitive person may have a friend who is stubborn and willful. This friend may want to go to a specific restaurant for dinner, while the HSP would rather cook dinner because they need to save money. If the friend blames the HSP for their feelings, they may say something like, "You never want to do what I want to do. You don't care that I've been looking forward to going to this restaurant all week." The HSP has to decide if that statement is actually true or if it's their friend's attempt to shed blame and emotional responsibility. The HSP's instinct may be to respond with, "I do care, I'm sorry... You know what? Let's go to the restaurant." But this leads to the continuation of a toxic cycle. The HSP's friend learns that they can always shed emotional responsibility, and the HSP develops the false belief that their feelings don't matter.

There's a better way to handle this situation involving a more realistic analysis on the HSP's part. If the highly sensitive person can realize, in the moment, that their friend was being somewhat manipulative, then they can lay the groundwork for a healthier solution to the conflict—one in which both parties take emotional responsibility. It may feel uncomfortable for the HSP to respond with a statement like, "I really need to cook dinner tonight but maybe we can go to the restaurant later this month, or you could go without me." However, this is really the best response because it is honest, and it teaches the HSP's friend an important lesson—that they cannot go through life blaming others for their feelings.

When HSPs feel that it is too painful to stick up for their own needs, they must remember that doing so helps all parties involved. When the HSP is happy and healthy, it creates room for their friends and loved ones to find health and happiness as well. That is what the HSP should remember when they feel torn between the truth and the feelings of another individual.

Again, highly sensitive people find great pleasure in being there for loved ones. They have a gift for knowing how other people feel, and they love to capitalize on that gift by providing their support and compassion. In essence, they love to feel needed. When highly sensitive people are able to lend their empathic gifts to others, it feels fulfilling and deeply rewarding. But this is exactly why HSPs should protect their inherent empathy. If they dole it out any time anyone is in need, the HSP will soon burn out and tarnish the gift that makes them so special. Instead, HSPs should honor their empathy through offering it only when it stems from genuine care. They should only offer it when there is no risk of their own feelings being jeopardized, and they should avoid people-pleasing as much as they can. People-pleasing takes the beauty out of the HSP's vast reservoir of empathy. It turns something precious into something to be taken advantage of. So, if you are a highly sensitive person yourself, protect and honor your gifts. Learn to say "no" when necessary. And remember that your needs are just as important as everyone else's.

Chapter Summary

- People-pleasing is often a product of a difficult upbringing. It's not so much a conscious choice as it is a habit developed from an unstable early home dynamic.

- If HSPs are used to narcissistic responses from loved ones, they'll learn to bottle up their emotions, reject their feelings as unimportant, and negate their intuitions. They'll also develop the belief that they must always obey the wishes of others or otherwise suffer. This is dangerous.

- Highly sensitive people should start with baby steps, and they shouldn't be too hard on themselves when they struggle with altering their people-pleasing habits.

- Experts suggest the implementation of four basic steps in order for highly sensitive people to avoid taking on the emotions of others. These steps include the following: evaluating your own needs, using your preferred mode of communication, maintaining boundaries over time, and holding responsibility only for yourself.

In the next chapter, you will learn how to manage depression and anxiety as a highly sensitive person so you can live your best, healthiest life.

Chapter Four

Managing Depression and Anxiety

---

*"There is nothing wrong with you if there are
times you get weighed down by the heaviness of
the suffering in the world."*
—Rachel Samson, Australian Psychologist

We have already discussed how highly sensitive people
are prone to overstimulation. Their nervous systems are
built in such a way that they can't help but absorb all of
the stimuli around them. They take in much more than
what meets the eye, and they don't have the same
barriers that other people have. Rather than
unconsciously rejecting certain energies from the

environment, HSPs absorb them and then process them with depth and consciousness, no matter how small or insignificant these energies may appear to others. Therefore, it's no surprise that highly sensitive people are especially prone to depression and anxiety. They walk around this world with porous skin, constantly soaking up the emotions and nuances around them. This allows them to see beneath the surface layer of things, but it also makes them easily vulnerable.

According to research, about 20 percent of people alive today are considered highly sensitive. However, about 50 percent of clients in therapy are distinguished as being highly sensitive people. This is true for two reasons, according to Julie Bjelland, a licensed psychotherapist in California. Highly sensitive people tend to be more interested in therapy and self-help, and they're also more likely to need therapy in the first place. HSPs tend to have higher levels of stress, depression, and anxiety, so of course they make up roughly half of the clients in therapy. Needless to say, highly sensitive individuals are susceptible to emotional overload of all sorts.

Depression

If someone close to an HSP is having a bad day, the HSP will feel that negativity, and more than likely, they will subconsciously internalize it. It is hard for a highly sensitive person to enjoy themselves and maintain a positive mood if the energy around them is negative. And the world is full of negativity, making HSPs an easy target for depression and anxiety.

Additionally, highly sensitive people tend to have vivid inner worlds. They're overthinkers and they can get lost in fantasies, but just as often, they get caught in mental spirals about how those around them are feeling. So, boundaries are essential, but so is self-awareness. Highly sensitive people feel everything very deeply. They fixate on their troubles and the larger troubles of the world. For this reason, HSPs need to find appropriate coping mechanisms to stabilize their often fluctuating emotions.

But there's another common source for an HSP's depression, and it has to do with acceptance. Many highly sensitive people grow up totally unaware of their sensitivities, or perhaps they're aware, but they lack the insight or vocabulary to define it. Again, many HSPs are raised in environments where their feelings aren't given voice, maybe due to a narcissistic parent, or maybe due to an unspoken agreement among the family. Regardless, acceptance and knowledge is essential if HSPs wish to heal from depression. Many highly sensitive people don't realize they're depressed until adulthood, often not until their late twenties. Furthermore, depression looks different for every highly sensitive person. Sometimes, it lingers under the surface throughout most of an HSP's life. Other times, it occurs more as a phase. However, it's important to realize that just because you are a highly sensitive person, you are not doomed to a life of depression. If you're an HSP, your sensitivity makes you more susceptible to taking on the heaviness of life, but that doesn't mean that you can't heal or manage depression the same way you can manage overstimulation.

Knowledge and self-awareness are key. If an HSP is unable to recognize their depression when it hits, then they are also unable to come up with a plan to make it better. When this happens, depression has the power to fester so that it is controlling the HSP when, really, it should be the other way around. But HSPs have the power to control their depression, or at least take steps to moderate it and work toward healing. The worst thing they can do is consistently force themselves into situations of overstimulation; this has the effect of pumping too much cortisol into the system which is how depression and anxiety manifest in the body.

Additionally, if a highly sensitive person is unaware of their deeply sensitive natures, they are more likely to criticize themselves when overwhelming emotions crop up. They may wonder things like, "Why can't I just be like everyone else?" If these kinds of feelings ruminate in the mind unchecked, they can snowball into irrational beliefs like, "There must be something wrong with me," or "Why do I get so nervous when everyone else seems just fine?" These kinds of beliefs are toxic for highly sensitive individuals. They can destroy their self-esteem and undoubtedly lead to depression. But, if HSPs can accept their sensitivities as a gift and commodity that needs to be protected, then they can shift their limiting beliefs and celebrate their sensitivities rather than condemn them.

Through healthy acknowledgment and acceptance, HSPs can orient their lives in a way that promotes peace and happiness while simultaneously guarding against overstimulation. That way, when HSPs do encounter triggers for depression, they know how to deal with it. They have tools to protect themselves and cultivate the best life possible. This looks different for each HSP, but it usually involves saying "no" to invitations that would prompt overstimulation, avoiding loud or noisy places, avoiding toxic work environments, etc.

If you're an HSP and do encounter depression, there are actions you can take to heal. It may not happen all at once, and it may take some solid commitment and work, but highly sensitive people actually have the power to heal quicker than non-HSPs in many cases. This is because something as simple as a beautiful song has the power to transport an HSP to a happier dimension. Highly sensitive people are also highly emotionally intelligent, making them very receptive to things like therapy and self-help.

So, if you're an HSP who has found yourself in a depressive funk, follow these guidelines to reorient yourself:

1.   Feel All the Feelings

First, it's important that you give yourself permission to feel all the feelings. It is quite impossible to heal if you can't first acknowledge and feel your emotions. Feeling the emotions is a sort of release for highly sensitive people, and it's impossible to move on to the next step until you process and release all the emotions. For some highly sensitive people, this may feel uncomfortable, especially if they were raised in homes where they had to suppress their emotions for the sake of the family. If this is the case, it may take some time and work to notice the feelings when they come up. If you're an HSP who is not used to acknowledging and releasing emotions, understand that it's an essential part of the healing process. Work on spending time with yourself. Notice how your body responds to the minor stresses of your day. Perhaps you can take ten minutes to sit in silence and notice where your mind goes. If you feel tension in your body, ask yourself about the source of that tension. By being fully in your body, you can learn to accept your feelings as they arrive. Then, you can begin the necessary work of feeling and releasing.

2.   Seek Help

Furthermore, if you are an HSP who is struggling with depression, it is wise to seek some form of help. In today's day and age, there are many options for professional emotional support and guidance. Therapy, for example, is more accessible than ever. You can meet with therapists remotely, over the computer, via text, or in the office the old-fashioned way. Or, if therapy feels too uncomfortable, you can also find assistance in professionals such as life coaches, healers, or even other HSPs on digital forums. There's never been more opportunity to seek professional help for mental health challenges, so why not take advantage? Generally, most HSPs enjoy the therapeutic process. It can be deeply fulfilling to have a safe space just for you, where you can cry and work through and release any emotions that you have neglected or bottled up. Sometimes, all it takes is a compassionate listener to make HSPs feel more accepted and less anxious. Professionals have the ability to find creative solutions that you may have otherwise never thought of. So, if you're an HSP who struggles with depression or anxiety, it's well advised that you seek some form of counseling. It absolutely has the power to change a highly sensitive person's life.

3. Educate Yourself

By the same token, it's also worthwhile to educate yourself on topics of mental health. The more you understand the nature of depression, why it occurs, and how to combat it, the more you'll be able to face it with confidence. Depression can feel shameful if you don't realize how common and natural it is. Through educating yourself, you can eradicate any sense of shame, and you can find creative solutions to depressive episodes.

So what exactly is depression? According to the American Psychiatric Association, it's a common and serious medical illness that negatively affects how you feel, the way you think, and how you act. It can affect your job performance and desire to participate in activities you enjoy. Symptoms include the following:

○ Sadness or living with depressive moods

○ Losing the ability to enjoy activities that used to offer joy

○ Loss of appetite and extreme weight loss or gain

○ Difficulty falling asleep or a propensity toward oversleeping

○ Loss of energy and constant feelings of depletion

○ Increase in purposeless physical activity (e.g., inability to sit still, pacing, handwringing) or slowed movements or speech (these actions must be severe enough to be observable by others)

○ Feelings of worthlessness or excessive guilt

○ Having trouble focusing or making decisions

○ Increased thoughts of death or suicide

This is just the tip of the iceberg when it comes to information on depression (Torres, 2020). Through just a bit of online research, you can learn what occurs in the brain, how many people experience depression, what generally triggers it, and so much more. I encourage this kind of research, especially for highly sensitive individuals, because it takes the stigma out of the equation. Additionally, it offers the ability to become self-aware, which is essential in terms of healing mental health issues.

1.   Establish a Self-Care Routine

After you've given yourself permission to feel your feelings, you've sought help, and you've educated yourself, you can establish a self-care routine that promotes a healthy balanced life. A healthy self-care routine can offer the foundation needed to decrease depressive episodes or even ward them off completely.

Your self-care routine should be specific to you and your personality. It will look different for every highly sensitive person. The important thing is that you identify what works best for you and stick with it. Whether it's a weekly bath, a daily journaling session, morning yoga, or nightly reading, self-care has the power to replace depression and anxiety with inner-peace and groundedness.

While self-care is meant to facilitate inner-peace and a general sense of homeostasis, there is another tip for overcoming depression which involves breaking out of your established routine. Believe it or not, experts suggest doing something challenging each week to create a healthier mental state. This is most easily accomplished once your self-care routine is firmly in place. With that foundation as support, you can challenge yourself to try new things. Through trying new things, you're bringing a new sense of spontaneity in your life. You're showing yourself that you have untapped potential and that the world is full of possibilities. You're also showing yourself that you can do hard things successfully, which is huge when it comes to improving self-esteem. Every time you challenge yourself, you're also investing in yourself. You're shaking things up and giving your life some much needed variety. Depression can grow worse if you continue to do the same things, the same way, every single day. But through making space for new challenges, you're inviting fresh energy into your daily existence. You're giving yourself the opportunity to show the world what you're made of. And after you challenge yourself more than a few times, you'll find that your confidence has increased—and so has your sense of purpose, presence, and spontaneity.

2. Fall in Love with the Present Moment

There's another habit that is useful to incorporate if you suffer from depression or anxiety. For some people, it is quite difficult to accomplish, but with a commitment to heal, you can become an expert at it. It involves falling in love with the present moment. Many highly sensitive people spend a great deal of time in their heads. They fixate on the future and their intuitive hunches about possible threats or on the past and their regrets. For this reason, mindfulness is important. But living in the present moment takes more than just mindfulness.

In order to truly find inner-peace, HSPs must learn not just to accept the present moment but to fall in love with it. Luckily, HSP's sensitive natures give them ample opportunities to fall in love with the present. If you're a highly sensitive person, it could be as simple as listening to your favorite song while you work or clean. It could be a focused attention on beautiful scenery, an acknowledgment of the beauty in nature during your commute to work. It could also be a prayer or a focused meditation session. More likely than not, you already have some experiences throughout your daily life where this comes naturally, but for dreamy HSPs, it's important to infuse life with as much appreciation for the present moment as possible. The more you're able to step back and enjoy reality just as it is, the more you'll be able to stop depressing thoughts before they arrive. It's also helpful in cultivating a gracious mindset. When you're tuned into life's beauty, you'll find that it's less necessary to seek escape through vices or negative thought spirals. You'll approach life with gratitude and acceptance, and eventually, you may find that there's little room for depression in your psyche.

3.   Follow a Life of Purpose

Finally, it's absolutely essential that highly sensitive people live a life of purpose. Because HSPs feel so deeply, they can't function in a life that is built around superficial concerns or goals. They need to feel like they are offering something to the world, and that the world has something to offer them as well. Depression is almost inevitable if an HSP is forced into a lifestyle that doesn't suit their sensitive nature. It can feel crippling and downright miserable.

Unfortunately, however, modern society isn't built to make HSPs a top priority. Highly sensitive people have needs that appear different from the average person, especially in consumerist cultures where there's such a focus on money and climbing the corporate ladder. Highly sensitive people have a spiritual need to experience life on a more profound level. They have to make decisions based on their soul's hunger for meaning. So, if they try to fit into a mold that doesn't align with their true desires, they'll quickly become depressed.

Now, it's also important to acknowledge that discovering one's purpose can take time. Sometimes, it takes many years for an HSP to discover their true vocation or the specific thing that really makes their heart sing. Nevertheless, highly sensitive people must give themselves permission to seek their purpose. They must offer themselves the freedom to follow their heart and live by their deepest, most spiritual truths. This is the only way HSPs can achieve the long-lasting inner peace they so desire.

Anxiety

Anxiety is also a common feeling and experience for highly sensitive people. HSPs tend to be more prone to anxiety for the same reasons they're more prone to depression. With a propensity toward overstimulation, it's all too easy to feel overwhelmed in crowded places or around loud noises and bright lights. But anxiety can stem from a lot of different things. It can manifest in stressful relationships, in the workplace, or even while driving to the grocery store. Every HSP experiences anxiety for different reasons and at different levels. But if you're a highly sensitive person who often feels anxious, it's important to acknowledge that feeling when it arrives, just like depression. Additionally, it's helpful to have coping mechanisms at your disposal whenever anxious feelings overwhelm the system. Just like anything else, awareness and coping strategies offer some semblance of control when your body may feel totally out of control. So how do you recognize anxiety when it arrives? What do the symptoms look like and feel like?

According to one psychologist, "You can recognise anxiety by that jittery, nervous feeling we all experience before a job interview or a first date. Our hands start sweating and our heart starts beating faster. Our mouth goes dry as our body becomes flooded with adrenaline, a hormone that is released when we are afraid. Anxiety makes it hard to concentrate, eat, and sleep and we become fixated on the issue that is causing us to feel anxious. We can easily begin to panic" (Ward, 2021). Certain scenarios, such as a first date or job interview, are likely circumstances for anxiety. It's natural to get nervous before a high-stakes situation. But for many HSPs, anxiety arrives when they least expect it, which can feel embarrassing and isolating. Still, it's important to understand that anxiety is natural, especially when your brain functions differently from that of the average person. If you're an HSP who often experiences anxiety, don't condemn yourself—that will only make the experience worse. Instead, recognize the feelings and remember to utilize your coping strategies:

1.   Learn to Cope with Anxious Feelings

The first step in learning to cope with anxious feelings is learning to recognize your body's anxious signals. This is different for everyone, but in most cases, it involves symptoms such as dry mouth, rapid beating heart, sweating, trembling, and overall feelings of weakness or fatigue. Mostly, though, it feels like jittery nerves. When HSPs feel this kind of sensation coming on, it's important that they recognize and acknowledge the signals from their bodies. It's important to realize that anxiety is just a feeling and a product of an overly sensitive nervous system. There's nothing wrong or bad about experiencing anxiety. According to the National Alliance on Mental Illness, over 40 million adults in the US experience anxiety regularly. So, if you are an HSP who often feels anxious, eliminate any and all judgment, and follow these steps to face your anxiety head-on.

2.   Face Your Fears

After recognizing your symptoms, you can also recognize that you have the power to conquer them, but it will require some self-compassion and practice. Most importantly, you need to muster the courage (as difficult as that can be) to face whatever it is that's frightening you. It's important to remember that whatever it is, it's not the end of the world. More than likely, once you face the fear head-on, you'll feel relieved after the whole event is over. It's easy to create scenarios of doom in our heads, especially for HSPs, with their vivid inner worlds. But more often than not, the fears that riddle your imagination are far less significant in reality. So, rather than running away or hiding from whatever it is that is prompting anxiety, acknowledge the feeling and then lean into it. Rip off the bandage. The more often you face your fears head-on, the more confidence you'll gain. Soon, you'll discover that anxiety is just a feeling— one that you have the power to conquer.

3.   Calm Your Body

When you're in the midst of an anxiety attack, there are certain things you can do to calm your body so that you have enough courage to face your fears. Breathing is massively important. Just a simple controlled inhale and exhale can do wonders for alleviating stress and anxiety. It's also helpful to ground yourself in reality. Try putting your hand on a nearby wall or sitting on the ground if you have the opportunity to do so and focus on the physical presence of your setting. These are simple reminders that anxiety is just a feeling. No matter how intense your fears may feel, you're still alive and breathing. The earth is still supporting you. This is just a moment in time. In the same vein, if you experience anxiety on a regular basis, you may consider relaxation techniques like meditation, yoga, exercise, or even playing calming music.

4.   Create Boundaries

If your intimate or personal relationships are causing anxiety, it may be a sign that you need to create stricter boundaries. Unfortunately, relationships are a common trigger for highly sensitive people. HSPs care so much about maintaining harmony and making others comfortable that they often feel extremely nervous when conflict inevitably ensues. People who are particularly aggressive are also a common source of anxiety for HSPs. Although an HSP's instinct may be to people-please and walk on eggshells when these kinds of situations arise, they should learn to create boundaries instead. If you're an HSP and have someone in your life who makes you feel anxious on a regular basis, consider the various ways you can protect yourself. It may be that you need to tell your friend or roommate you need more privacy. Or perhaps you have to stand up to a coworker. No matter what the issue is, boundaries are key. It may feel uncomfortable to state your boundaries clearly, especially when the relationship is unstable, but it's the major method HSPs have to protect themselves. As stated in the previous chapter, once those boundaries are created, HSPs can discover a new sense of confidence and trust in themselves. They then feel that they have more control over their anxiety and their ability to achieve inner peace.

If you're a highly sensitive person who is prone to depression and anxiety, there are still ways to live a happy and healthy life. Remember, your sensitivity is an asset that needs to be protected. Your sensitive nature is a gift, and every gift does come with a cost, but that doesn't mean you can't control the negative side-effects. Many psychologists believe that depressive episodes are actually necessary, that they function almost like a purge.

Sometimes, you have to fully experience a negative emotion before you can let go and heal.

Don't be afraid to request medical help if nothing else is working for you. Unfortunately, there's still a stigma against medication, but many people find it incredibly helpful. Some people can't create the proper chemicals in their brains naturally—they need medicinal help to achieve a stable mental state. There shouldn't be any shame surrounding this. If you need prescription medicine to feel better, ask your psychiatrist for a diagnosis and get whatever help you need.

Ultimately, the best thing you can do as an HSP is accept your negative feelings when they arrive. With the opportunity to feel epic highs comes the propensity for lows as well. So don't fight it. It's better to accept yourself as the sensitive and deeply empathetic person you are. And with some coping strategies in place, you never have to feel out of control. Take time to feel. There is always something to be gained from accessing your emotions, even the negative ones. Embrace the experience and the gifts that result from it.

Chapter Summary

- It is hard for a highly sensitive person to enjoy themselves and maintain a positive mood if the energy around them is negative. The world is full of negativity, making HSPs an easy target for depression and anxiety.

- If a highly sensitive person is unaware of their deeply sensitive natures, they are more likely to criticize themselves when overwhelming emotions crop up.

- If you often experience depression as a highly sensitive person, you should give yourself permission to feel all the feelings, seek help, educate yourself, establish a self-care routine, fall in love with the present moment, and follow a life of purpose.

- With a propensity toward overstimulation, it's all too easy to feel overwhelmed in crowded places or around loud noises and bright lights. But anxiety can stem from a lot of different things. It can manifest in stressful relationships, in the workplace, or even while driving to the grocery store.

- The best way to handle anxiety as an HSP is through learning to cope, facing your fears, calming your body, and creating boundaries.

In the next chapter, you will learn how to navigate social relationships successfully as a highly sensitive person.

CHAPTER FIVE

Social Relationships

"As a highly sensitive person, every little thing elicits a strong reaction in me."
—Tracy M. Kusmierz, Communications Manager at Not for Profit Organization

For highly sensitive people, social relationships are a source of both euphoria and anxiety. Due to their deep feeling nature, HSPs crave connection more than anything else. The experience of feeling seen and understood by another individual is like the greatest drug in the world. Just think about it: the experience of love and connection is already a massively powerful feeling for the average individual. When you experience love and connection as a highly sensitive person, that already powerful sensation is exacerbated. It can only be described as transcendent. However, due to the epic stakes of social relationships, they also have the power to send HSPs into a negative tailspin. But with healthy awareness, highly sensitive people can enjoy the heights of their connections without suffering the toxic lows.

Boundaries are the key word when it comes to successful social relationships, and this is especially true for highly sensitive individuals. Boundaries protect both individuals within the partnership. They eliminate the risk of codependency and save the HSP from getting lost in a toxic cycle of people-pleasing. The nature of the boundaries might look different depending on the relationship and people involved, but nevertheless, boundaries are always necessary. The more confident HSPs become in enforcing those boundaries, the more successful their relationships become. Relationships thrive on a foundation of mutual respect. In order to feel respected as a person, you need to have your boundaries respected first and foremost.

We already discussed some ways you can enforce boundaries, but it really can't be emphasized enough. Since highly sensitive people are so empathetic and motivated to help others, they have to practice self-awareness and learn to protect themselves against people who might take advantage of their helpful nature. Combine this with the fact that HSPs are overly forgiving and often feel a need to prove themselves, and you end up with a person who is a magnet for toxic leeches. But that doesn't have to be the case. Boundaries protect HSPs. They're an essential safety net. But often, it's difficult to determine what boundaries should look like until the HSP has already experienced a fair share of heartache. Are you a highly sensitive person who has felt like a doormat in some of your friendships? Have you ever felt like you give and give but don't receive nearly as much in return? Have you ever felt like you're always the one apologizing or accommodating while your needs are being neglected? If you've answered "yes" to any of these questions, then you're already on your way to identifying where you need boundaries.

Take a moment and think about the situations that make you feel most neglected, overlooked, or used. How can you use those situations as a frame of reference for healthy boundaries? If you often feel taken advantage of when a friend wants to hang out every night with no consideration for your need for solitude, then that's a boundary you need to enforce. Once you recognize that you need alone time, you can state that need clearly. Then, you have the ability to gauge the respect levels in your relationship. If your friend respects your boundaries, they're a friend worth keeping. If they don't, you should probably consider making new friends instead. As an HSP, it's useful to reflect on previous relationships throughout your life.

Follow this exercise to gauge respect levels in your relationships:

-   Close your eyes and meditate on the relationships that have made you feel safe and secure.

-   Once you've identified a few people, try doing the same thing but with people who have made you feel exhausted or insecure.

Thinking about the way your relationships make you feel can help you identify where boundaries need to be enforced. That way, you can be more selective when making friends in the future, and you can state your needs clearly from the jump, with confidence and clarity.

For some highly sensitive people, social relationships can feel overly burdensome. If you're an HSP who has consistently been hurt or taken advantage of in personal relationships, you may feel less inclined to go out into the world and seek new friendships. However, friendships can be a deeply fulfilling and necessary part of life for HSPs. Again, HSPs need to experience connection. They need to feel seen and understood in order to thrive and live a healthy, happy life. Rather than avoid friendships, they should choose their friends wisely because a good friend to an HSP has the power to pull them out of their shells, make them feel supported, and lift them out of negative emotional spirals. Good friends fulfill an extraordinary purpose for sensitive folk. Plus, they offer a change of pace from romantic relationships. Romantic relationships are equally fulfilling, but they can't possibly meet every one of the HSP's needs. With a healthy amount of solid friendships, HSPs can build a support system to lean on when romantic relationships verge on codependency.

High Sensitivity and Introversion

There's another important point to consider when it comes to highly sensitive people and their ability to make and keep friends. The majority of HSPs are deeply introverted people. This means they don't always feel comfortable approaching new people with confidence. The psychological definition for introversion is, "the tendency to be concerned with one's own thoughts and feelings rather than with external things." This focus on internal thought makes it difficult to approach people without overthinking. Plus, HSPs are deeply concerned with making other people feel comfortable. They may get too "in their heads" about making new friends, even when the opportunity presents itself. But this doesn't mean that highly sensitive introverts can't make new friends. They simply have to find natural ways to do so.

Many highly sensitive people make friends easily when they can meet others through pre-established friendships. This lessens the pressure and makes the whole process more organic. The same goes for clubs or activities where introverted HSPs can meet like-minded individuals. Through bonding over a shared interest, there's less chance of getting caught in superficial conversations, which is an HSP's worst nightmare. Finally, some introverts prefer meeting people online, where they can communicate without the anxiety that comes from real-life conversation.

No matter your method for making friends as a timid HSP, you should be patient with yourself. Understand that many people are introverts, and your shy and gentle qualities are desired in friendships. At the same time, practice discretion when choosing your friends. If you're an introverted HSP, you want to have people in your life who understand and celebrate your quiet, reflective nature. Anyone who isn't willing to do that is not a friend worth having.

Empathy

Whether you're introverted or extroverted, if you're highly sensitive, you're also most likely highly empathic. HSPs are known for being overly empathetic. They can understand how others feel, not just intellectually but also on a feeling level. They can quite literally absorb the emotions of others and experience them as if they are their own. This is a gift because it allows HSPs to relate to others, form intimate connections, and lend a helping hand when need be. However, too much empathy can also have negative consequences, and HSPs understand this better than anyone else. When you're constantly feeling what other people feel, and taking responsibility for those feelings at the same time, you can drive yourself crazy trying to facilitate harmony. You can find yourself in a vicious cycle of trying to guess how your loved one will react to every single thing you say or do. This is a problem because it doesn't allow for authenticity and it also means the HSP is constantly on edge.

Relationships to Avoid

Empathy is one of the key ingredients to successful relationships of any kind, but too much empathy has the power to destroy relationships if it leads to a lopsided dynamic. For example, if one person within the relationship is overly empathetic while the other lacks empathy, it is impossible to have an equal partnership with even give and take. Obviously, this type of dynamic leads to the highly sensitive individual feeling taken advantage of, which is exactly what HSPs need to avoid. HSPs should offer empathy in their friendships but only as much as they receive in return. They must practice self-awareness and protect their empathy so that it deepens their relationships instead of having the opposite effect. This takes practice, but with honest self-awareness, HSPs can strike the balance necessary to use empathy to their advantage. Plus, HSPs have the special ability to appreciate their relationships more than most. They have more to gain psychologically and emotionally than the average person in a relationship. They just have to be careful with how they give out their empathy; not everyone is deserving of HSP's special gift.

Shallow Relationships

With all that empathy and sensitivity, it's no wonder that highly sensitive people thrive in healthy relationships built on authenticity. But HSPs are a rare breed. Most people don't possess the same capacity for empathy and sensitivity that they do. This is another reason why highly sensitive people struggle when it comes to social relationships. For HSPs, shallow relationships are simply a waste of time. Small talk is boring and pointless, and ego relationships don't do anything for them.

Because HSPs thrive on deep authentic connection, they often feel misunderstood. If they go to a party where everyone is discussing trivial topics, they'll easily feel out of place, like the odd man out. Instead of allowing this basic truth to make you feel defeated, you should simply avoid shallow relationships if you're a highly sensitive person. There are plenty of people who also detest artificiality, and those are the people HSPs should surround themselves with. If you're an HSP, don't let your desire for deep connection make you feel weird or abnormal. There are plenty of people who will understand you and value your need for depth. The more you eliminate and shy away from superficial people, the more you'll open up the space for deep and fulfilling connections. Don't waste your time with anything else.

Judgmental Friends

By the same token, highly sensitive people should do whatever they can to avoid judgemental friends. Self-acceptance should be a top priority for HSPs, and any threat against that needs to be removed without question. Therefore, HSPs should avoid judgmental people at all costs. HSPs tend to feel judged because, for the most part, they weren't allowed to own their sensitivities as children. For this reason, they take judgment much harder than the average person. They often lack the ability to say, "Well that's just a harsh judgment. I don't care what they think." Instead, they have a tendency to take on the judgments of others, internalizing it until they become resentful and angry. Many HSPs also struggle with self-esteem, and harsh judgments don't do much to improve this area. If you're a highly sensitive person and find yourself feeling judged by those closest to you, be honest with yourself and identify if those judgments are fair. More likely than not, they're just biased projections that threaten to hurt you and ruin your confidence. You don't need to give these people the time of day. If you're feeling overly judged, set some boundaries and allow yourself to be yourself. The people who accept you will come into your life and celebrate your uniqueness with love and understanding.

Overly Demanding Friends

There's another common type of friend that HSPs have a tendency to attract. Whether it's due to HSP's high levels of empathy or often introverted natures, overly demanding people flock to highly sensitive people. This is especially true of young HSPs who lack the insight to appropriately suss people out. These HSPs are eager to please, so of course, they attract friends who have high expectations and a sometimes demanding personality. If you're an HSP who has found yourself in a toxic friendship with too many demands, it's best to draw strict boundaries or end the friendship.

Again, HSPs would bend over backward for the people they love and cherish. But not everyone is deserving of their giving and generous natures. Highly sensitive people should reserve their generosity for those who truly deserve it. Otherwise, they'll end up feeling like a doormat in an unbalanced relationship. Be honest with yourself when you consider the give and take of your friendships. Is your friend giving you the same care and support that you give them? Sometimes, it's easy to convince yourself that things are balanced when they're actually not. If you notice that you're feeling resentful toward your friend, that's a sign that things are out of balance, even if you can convince yourself that your friend actually means well.

Sometimes it's hard to measure the give and take in these kinds of relationships. For example, you may be an HSP who is quiet and somewhat reserved, but whenever your friend needs your help, you jump to their rescue, whether it's driving them when they need a ride, listening whenever they need a shoulder to cry on, or following along with whatever activities they want to do. Essentially, you may be the type of friend who's always available, and although you may not throw them parties or shower them with gifts, you're still a rock for your friend, one who deserves much appreciation. On the other hand, maybe your friend is the type of person who throws you parties and showers you with gifts. This is a common dynamic: one friend offers love in the form of emotional support and constant availability, while the other offers more superficial displays of care, such as buying them food or other material objects. In this example, it may be quite easy for the HSP to make excuses for the friend. "They're so generous," the HSP may think. "They always lend me money when I need it and they buy me coffee whenever they go to Starbucks. So why do I get so randomly angry at them?" the HSP may wonder.

Rather than attempting to reconcile this conundrum by making excuses for the friend, HSPs should recognize resentment when it arrives. Resentment is usually a sign that things are out of balance. More often than not, it's hard to distinguish which party is giving more to the friendship, so it may be better to think about the form of love you need. Is your friend giving you the type of love and form of care that you desire? If the answer is no, you should be honest with your friend about your needs or consider seeking new friendships.

Highly sensitive people make amazing friends. They're empathetic, genuinely caring, patient, and understanding. If you're a highly sensitive person, know your worth and understand that your friendship is a prize. You don't have to put up with draining or demanding friends. Look for relationships that offer an equal give and take and make you feel seen and valued. Once HSPs value their worth as amazing friends, they can experience profound and even life-changing relationships built on mutual respect and growth.

Highly sensitive people have a lot to gain through social relationships. As humans in general, we can't have all of our needs fulfilled through one person alone. Since HSPs are prone to codependency in romance, they should seek friendships that support and nourish them. The more people they can count on for emotional support, the better. When HSPs have a plethora of quality friends to choose from, they're less likely to become codependent in romantic relationships and they're more likely to live life with confidence and high self-esteem. Friendships are important for everyone, but they're especially important for HSPs who find special value in authentic connection.

Chapter Summary

- When it comes to social relationships, boundaries protect both individuals within the partnership. They eliminate the risk of codependency and save the HSP from getting lost in a toxic cycle of people-pleasing.

- It's important to gauge respect levels within your relationships.

- Avoid falling into vicious cycles of trying to guess how your loved one will react to every single thing you say or do. This is a problem because it doesn't allow for authenticity, and it also means the HSP is constantly on edge.

- HSPs should also avoid shallow relationships, judgmental friends, and overly demanding friends.

- When HSPs have a plethora of quality friends to choose from, they're less likely to become codependent in romantic relationships and they're more likely to live life with confidence and high self-esteem.

In the next chapter, you will learn how to navigate intimate and romantic relationships as a highly sensitive individual.

Chapter Six

Close and Romantic Relationships

"Highly sensitive beings suffer more but they also love harder, dream wider and experience deeper horizons and bliss. When you're sensitive, you're alive in every sense of this word in this wildly beautiful world. Sensitivity is your strength. Keep soaking in the light and spreading it to others."
—Victoria Erickson, author of Edge of Wonder

Many people claim that romantic relationships are especially challenging for highly sensitive people, and perhaps there is some truth to that. However, HSPs also have the capacity to master romantic relationships better than anyone else. No one understands what is required to make a close relationship successful better than someone who is deeply sensitive. Highly sensitive people understand nuances, and they have high levels of emotional intelligence and empathy. With a bit of insight and maturity, HSPs can have more successful and fulfilling romantic connections than anyone else.

Many of the challenges that HSPs experience in intimacy are rooted in the need for acceptance. As stated previously, highly sensitive people sometimes have trouble accepting themselves for the deeply emotional and passionate people they are. When HSPs can't accept their sensitive natures, either because they were taught to repress them or because they simply haven't been given the opportunity to do so, they often attract partners who don't accept them either. But when HSPs accept and embrace their sensitivities, they tend to attract partners who do the same. So, coming to terms with their emotional predispositions will always prove advantageous. As the saying goes, you can't love someone else until you learn to love yourself. This is just as true for highly sensitive people as it is for the average person.

Highly sensitive people experience every subtlety at a

higher octave. A smile from a stranger, for example, will penetrate deeper for an HSP than an average person who may not even notice the smiling fellow. HSPs are more vulnerable to sensory overload and environmental stimulation in general. So it's no surprise that love and romance mark a particularly overwhelming experience for highly sensitive people. This is both good and challenging. Romance tends to be an overwhelmingly intense experience even for the average person, so when you consider the fact that HSPs have an irregular nervous system and are more prone to overstimulation, you see why HSPs fall in love hard. Even a casual romance can send the HSP into overdrive. They have the capacity to idealize and fall in love with someone over the simplest of gestures. In general, HSPs have a tendency to romanticize even the smallest events in life. So when they fall in love, the experience is nothing short of earth-shattering.

Craving Connection While Fearing Intimacy

The propensity for overstimulation in love is just as

thrilling as it is scary. When a highly sensitive person is first caught up in early romance, they have the power to feel profoundly euphoric. They may feel as though all of their problems are miniscule, that they are healed from every trauma they've ever endured, and that everything in life will be okay so long as they have the love of their partner. They experience romance at a fairytale level, where they are forever teenagers falling in love for the first time. In essence, HSPs are hopeless romantics. Non-HSPs could easily feel jealous of this. If love is like the most epic drug on earth, why wouldn't we all hope to experience the highest dosage of it? But if you're a highly sensitive person who has fallen in and out of love, you know that there is more to it than rainbows and butterflies. With all that intensity also comes the potential for devastation. Highly sensitive people must learn to protect themselves from the onslaught of emotions and confusion that intimacy brings.

As stated previously, highly sensitive people tend to have vivid inner worlds. They have strong intuitive faculties and can imagine great potential in any given situation. This is why HSPs have a habit of idealizing love. They often see things for more than the literal representation in reality; they see rich possibilities. They imagine potential and easily get lost in fantasy. This is what makes HSPs so creative and wise, but it's also the source of much heartache in love. If an HSP falls in love with the idea of a person, for example, this can be devastating. It sets the partner up for unrealistic expectations, and it can be disappointing when the idealized love doesn't live up to the HSP's perfect image in their heads. And, of course, it makes endings that much more difficult.

When you fall in love harder than the average person, you also have the capacity for deeper and more long-lasting heartbreak. There's often nothing worse than the first time a highly sensitive person gets their heart broken. It feels like the end of the world. But these moments act as valuable lessons for HSPs. The more they learn about their specific tendencies and idiosyncrasies in love, the better they can protect themselves in future relationships. For HSPs, self-protection in love is more complicated than an attempt to monitor intense emotions. That's because while most highly sensitive people crave love, many also fear intimacy. This makes the whole experience complicated, not just for the HSP but also for the HSP's partner.

This goes back to the issue of HSPs craving connection while lacking the tools to bring it about. For highly sensitive people, human connection is the most fulfilling experience in the world. But most HSPs, due to their upbringings, may not have been given the tools to achieve connection organically, especially intimate connection. Therefore, intimacy is a complicated matter for HSPs. On the one hand, they need it, and on the other hand, they have no idea what it looks like. This leads to feelings of inadequacy and fear. It's all too common for HSPs to fall in love hard only to feel disappointed when the initial heights of romance subside. That's typically when fear creeps in. And there's no greater adversary to love than fear.

Fears of intimacy can no doubt sabotage a perfectly good relationship, but that doesn't mean that HSPs are doomed if they have trouble being vulnerable. Vulnerability is scary for nearly everyone, but it's especially scary for highly sensitive people who are already more vulnerable to begin with. The various reasons why HSPs may fear intimacy look different for everyone. A majority of the time, HSPs fear that they will become too engulfed in the relationship and may lose themselves entirely if they expose it all. This is a normal fear to have, especially when you consider how generous and loyal HSPs tend to be. Highly sensitive people are more than willing to go the extra mile for their loved ones, which can easily lead to codependency or loss of self. But HSPs have the ability to strike a proper balance. With practice and awareness, they can learn to be totally vulnerable without fearing engulfment or enmeshment.

The more HSPs accept themselves and exercise self-love, the less likely they are to fear intimacy or enter codependent relationships. Self-care is also essential here. When highly sensitive people are able to feel comfortable in their independence, they're less inclined to seek out relationships that engulf them. But there's another common reason why HSPs fear intimacy that's quite different from fear of engulfment. Many HSPs had childhoods where they didn't receive enough attention or the right form of love they needed. Many may have felt abandoned or neglected in their early home environment, which leads to a fear of abandonment in adulthood. Of course, this also causes anxiety in intimate relationships. The more HSPs are desperate for commitment or stability, the more they may unconsciously drive their partners away—which is the opposite result the HSP is looking for.

Additionally, if a highly sensitive person is dating someone who lacks sensitivity, they may feel like a burden or like their emotions are too much for their overly detached partner. This can then lead to the HSP feeling deeply misunderstood and insecure. They may try to repress their feelings and please their partner, hoping to earn a "happily ever after." This never ends well. Instead of getting lost in partners who don't have the capacity or willingness to understand the HSP, highly sensitive people should opt for partners who *do* understand. This becomes easier when the HSP has enough awareness and confidence to accept their sensitive natures. When they accept themselves, they can attract and even seek out relationship partners who value and understand their deep emotions. They can communicate their needs honestly without feeling like their needs are "too much." This is how healthy HSP relationships develop.

What to Look for in a Partner

The more experience highly sensitive people have in the dating world, the more they're able to recognize with accuracy who would be a good match and who simply wouldn't fit the bill. It's not uncommon for HSPs to date the wrong type of partner, sometimes over and over again, before they realize what it is they need. Highly sensitive people can function well in relationships with non-highly sensitive people, but they have to ensure that their partner understands them and accepts them. They have to feel that their partner embraces their emotions and is willing to support them. When HSPs date less sensitive people and that understanding isn't there, it can lead to resentment and confusion. The HSP may have trouble respecting the less sensitive partner, even if they can't consciously understand why. When this occurs, they lose intimacy and progress within the relationship.

Highly sensitive people must first gain an understanding of their sensitive natures. Then they must find the courage to articulate their needs based on their understanding. If their partner then rejects their needs, which they very well may do, the HSP needs to have the strength to walk away. It gets easier with time. Eventually, highly sensitive people can date with an understanding that not everyone is perfect for them. There are people out there who will find the HSP's sensitivities beautiful. They will want to emotionally support them, even if they're not super sensitive themselves. Once HSPs understand that this is the type of partner they deserve, they can practice discretion when dating and won't lose themselves in one-sided relationships. If you're an HSP who longs for intimacy, don't be afraid to state your needs, and don't be afraid to walk away if your needs aren't being respected.

Relationships with Narcissists

When highly sensitive people are dating without awareness and acceptance, they tend to attract individuals who lack the capacity to understand and embrace their emotions. This can be disastrous. The opposite of a highly sensitive person is a person who lacks empathy entirely. HSPs have a tendency to attract a specific type of person when they lack self-acceptance—the HSP's opposite: the narcissist.

Narcissists love highly sensitive people because they're forgiving and understanding. It's all too common for HSPs to find themselves in relationships with narcissists. Of course, narcissists also lack empathy, so they make a horrible match for HSPs. But so long as HSPs can spot the warning signs, they can avoid unempathetic partners, as well as the toxic dynamic that comes with them.

It's worth exploring what the dynamic between a narcissist and an HSP looks like so that you may learn how to spot the red flags. Narcissists like to shower their HSP partners with love in the early stages of the relationship. They find a lot of gratification from the early romance period because their egos are being stroked and they feel as though they've finally found someone who worships them the way they expect to be worshiped. It's the perfect recipe for disaster because HSPs are more than happy to go out of their way for those they love. Eventually, narcissists pick up on the HSP's overly generous nature and consciously or subconsciously decide to take advantage of it. They become demanding and controlling, often using tactics such as harsh criticism and manipulation to gain a sense of superiority over the vulnerable HSP.

As this goes on, the HSP starts to lose themselves in the relationship. They may experience gaslighting and other forms of manipulation which render them powerless. Narcissists have impenetrable egos. They don't have the capacity to put their own feelings aside for the sake of another person, even someone they "love." As hard as the HSP may try, there's simply no getting through to their narcissistic partners. At a certain point, a cycle begins in which the narcissist demands more and more from the HSP, and the HSP does whatever they can to please, but they always inevitably fail. There's no pleasing a narcissist. The only person who can help a narcissist is the narcissist themself.

As criticism and impossible expectations continue, the HSP may realize that the relationship is abusive. This is where the HSP has a choice. They can either leave the narcissist or try to get the narcissist to admit to being abusive; this takes time, however. If you're an HSP who is in the throes of an abusive, narcissistic relationship, it is well advised to end the relationship immediately. More likely than not, the narcissist will never own up to their abusive behaviors because those admissions are too big a threat to their fragile ego. This is a difficult lesson for HSPs. If they fall victim to abuse in their adult relationships, they should take it as an opportunity to learn just how emotionally strong they are.

Relationships Involving Two HSPs

What if a highly sensitive person were to date the narcissist's opposite? What would happen if two highly sensitive people entered a relationship with each other? This may seem like the perfect recipe for understanding and harmony, and in many ways, it is. But just like anything else, these kinds of relationships have their challenges as well.

When two HSPs enter a relationship together, it can feel like magic, especially in the beginning. Both individuals are so in-tune with one another that it can feel like both people are one. Or at least, it can feel like they both share the same brain. Communication can be easier than relationships containing just one HSP because there's an intrinsic understanding of one another and a desire to get at each other's souls as well. Both people will probably feel seen in the eyes of the other, which is a desirable feeling for highly sensitive people.

Additionally, when two HSPs fall in love, there is much to bond and connect over. Both people may have a special connection to the arts and creativity. Both enjoy deep and often philosophical conversations. And both love to show affection and appreciation. Furthermore, both individuals are deeply concerned with the needs of the other, constantly checking in with each other and making sure both parties are satisfied. With all this being said, two HSPs certainly have the capacity to experience a kind of soulmate fusion. They think similarly, want the same things, and are eager to connect in a profound way. So what could possibly go wrong?

Love between two HSPs may look perfect on paper, but in reality, there are certain challenges to look out for. A relationship between two highly sensitive individuals means double the emotional heights, but also double the emotional lows. Basically, when one HSP is having a bad day, it will affect the other HSP, and vice versa. It can be difficult to detach in a relationship like this. Both HSPs may feel a special responsibility to support the other, which can lead to constant emotional entanglement. It can feel impossible to detach from the constant highs and lows. Also, both individuals are quick to feel responsible for the other's feelings. If one person is feeling down, the other person will feel like they must do something to fix it. They will probably feel as though they can't enjoy themselves until their partner is feeling good again. And the following week, the cycle may repeat itself, but this time, with the other individual feeling depressed. You can see how this can be draining, especially if there is a lack of awareness and personal responsibility.

Additionally, because HSPs are masters at picking up subtleties, there's very little that can be swept under the rug in this kind of relationship. In fact, it may be hard to relax because both individuals are just *that* in tune with one another. Even the slightest shift in energy could lead to emotional conversations about why the

HSP is intuiting negativity from the other HSP. When an HSP is in a relationship with a non-HSP, however, there's more room for light exchange and more of an ability to let things go and move on. With two HSPs, everything needs to be addressed immediately, which can get draining for both people involved.

There's also the likelihood that two HSPs will put so much emphasis on peace and harmony that they won't want to address the tiny ruptures that inevitably come up, even though they know they have to. Addressing emotions needs to be a common activity in a relationship between two HSPs. If both individuals prefer to avoid conflict, then resentment can build, and the relationship can become awkward. In turn, it will suffer. If you're an HSP who is in a relationship with another HSP, make sure that you approach conflict head-on. Don't run away from it, even if it feels uncomfortable. Highly sensitive people need to respect and experience their emotions, and the same goes for any partner of a highly sensitive person.

However, it is possible for two HSPs to thrive in union. If both are willing to only take responsibility for their own emotions, they can experience a form of closeness that is unprecedented while also learning the value of self-sufficiency in the process. This pair can experience an evolved form of love where both parties are emotionally strong and considerate of one another. But both must be willing to put in the work, and both must have a passion and willingness to go to the depths together. According to Dr. Elaine Aron, author of *The Highly Sensitive Person in Love*, HSPs can thrive in any relationship, both with other HSPs and non-HSPs, but she argues that a relationship between two HSPs may have a slight advantage. She states:

"The 'mixed couple' must learn to really believe that they experience the world quite differently. That's difficult because we all tend to assume everyone experiences things the way we do. So the first task is a deep acceptance that the other person's experience is real and valid. They can't help it. Then, I think you have to grieve that you didn't get everything in your partner, but then we never do. One counselor said, 'When you choose a partner, you choose a set of problems.' It's only in the movies or in dreams that we meet someone who is both an HSP and a non-HSP at once. After you accept and grieve, the two of you can get creative about how to enjoy each other and do things together. The danger is the subtle contempt one can feel for someone not like ourselves. The HSP may find the non-HSP a bit shallow or clueless, while benefiting from the non-HSPs ability to handle a lot more and protect the HSP. The non-HSP may subtly think the HSP is weak or self-absorbed. For example, HSPs need more time alone. The non-HSP may feel rejected, but also may feel that that behavior is selfish."

So either way, there are certain challenges to be aware of. It's probably best that HSPs keep their options open when it comes to finding true love. It's not wise to close yourself off to one individual simply because they're not an HSP. The same goes for other highly sensitive people. Instead, be honest with yourself and be honest about your needs. Once you understand your needs and know your worth, you will find the right person. The most important thing to do is make sure you never settle and always put yourself first. Highly sensitive people are well equipped for deep and meaningful long-lasting relationships. They know how to love and care for others, much more than most people, so if you're an

HSP who is looking for that special someone, protect your sensitivities and let your natural gifts radiate with confidence.

Chapter Summary

- When HSPs can't accept their sensitive natures, either because they were taught to repress them or because they simply haven't been given the opportunity to do so, they often attract partners who don't accept them either.

- The more HSPs are desperate for commitment or stability, the more they may unconsciously drive their partners away.

- Highly sensitive people must choose partners who embrace their emotions and are willing to support them. When highly sensitive people date less sensitive people and that understanding isn't there, it can lead to resentment and confusion.

- The opposite of a highly sensitive person is a person who lacks empathy entirely. HSPs have a tendency to attract that type of person when they lack self-acceptance. This person comes in the form of the narcissist.

- Relationships between two HSPs may seem like the perfect recipe for mutual understanding and depth, but there are certain challenges as well, like an overemphasis on the heavier aspects of life.

In the next chapter, you will learn how to thrive at work as a highly sensitive person.

CHAPTER SEVEN

Thriving at Work

"Sensitive people like a slower pace of life. We like pondering all our options before making a decision and regularly reflecting on our experiences. We hate busy schedules and rushing from one event to the next."
—Jenn Granneman, author at Introvert, Dear

Work can be a tricky area to navigate as a highly sensitive person. For many HSPs, the chaotic corporate world can be a source of constant stress and anxiety. Our modern society relies on "hustle culture" and fast-paced results in order to thrive. HSPs tend to prefer a slower pace. They enjoy life's smaller, more intimate moments. Although they can be competitive and highly ambitious, they're generally not desperate to climb the corporate ladder or find the next networking opportunity. HSPs tend to be motivated by people more than anything else, as well as moments that provide a peaceful kind of joy and serenity. For this reason, HSPs often feel misunderstood in the workplace. Their gifts aren't always appreciated in our current society's rapid and aggressive work culture. They can feel dejected when it comes to finding their unique place within the larger collective. Luckily, though, our society is becoming more aware of sensitivities than ever before. And with a little bit of self-acceptance and honesty, HSPs can thrive in a workplace that makes them feel comfortable and fully embraced for the sensitive individuals that they are.

There are many different fields where sensitivity is needed and where it can actually serve as an asset toward success. But some HSPs may not even realize that those kinds of opportunities are out there. For example, if you're an HSP who has lived most of your life totally unaware of your deep sensitivities, you may have no idea that you would be happier as a therapist than as an advertising agent. Perhaps your parents want you to pursue a specific field of work, and you figure they know

113

what's best. It can be disappointing, though, when the HSP actually enters the workforce and finds themselves miserable. Every HSP is different, of course, but for the most part, highly sensitive people need to participate in work that nourishes their souls, provides inner meaning, and helps other people in some way. If they find themselves acting as just another cog in the machine, they will quickly grow depressed. Again, HSPs need to live a life of purpose. Finding a true vocation that fills the highly sensitive individual with passion should be a top priority.

At the same time, HSPs mustn't put too much pressure on themselves. Finding your true purpose takes time, and it's okay to try many different things before you settle into one specific career. It's okay to be patient with yourself in this regard. Still, if you're an HSP who is struggling to find purpose, don't settle into a job or lifestyle that leaves you feeling anxious. There have never been more opportunities for highly sensitive people to build a life of comfort and meaning. Don't betray your needs for the sake of money or approval. When you're committed to your purpose, everything else falls into place.

There are two distinct issues that often arise when it comes to finding career success and happiness, and this is especially true for highly sensitive people. The first issue involves achieving a lifestyle that promotes peace, and the second involves finding a career that provides a sense of purpose. Typically, one of these issues has to take priority before both can find resolution. So what do HSPs need in terms of lifestyle in order to feel secure and happy? This may look different depending on whether the HSP in question is an introvert or an extrovert, but typically, HSPs require a peaceful life where they can feel valued and also take quiet time for reflection when necessary.

Work Environments to Avoid as an HSP

We've already discussed the various ways highly sensitive people are different from the average person; many become overwhelmed in crowded places, for example, or overstimulated by harsh lighting or loud noises. Obviously, work that involves talking to a lot of people in harsh conditions would not fare well for most HSPs. Highly sensitive people are also more prone to internalizing criticisms than the average person. They tend to get nervous with a head over their shoulders, and they need lots of time to think deeply about things before moving on to the next thing. A rapid-paced office job would not be very ideal, nor would any work that involves a lot of aggressive personalities.

Most highly sensitive people prefer jobs where they can work from home in solitude or work with people in a one-on-one capacity. Small talk can be incredibly draining for HSPs, so they should avoid jobs that place them in the throes of superficial conversation. Fields such as telemarketing, sales, and advertising are some of the worst careers for highly sensitive people, not only because they tend to be competitive and lacking in depth, but also because they involve a lot of harsh conversations and the necessity to be pushy. If HSPs do decide to work in a public place, they should avoid environments with toxic personalities. Some HSPs can really thrive when working in small offices with people they truly love. If they work closely with people who make them feel misunderstood or exhausted, they should find a better option. It's not worth it to spend the majority of your day feeling anxious or uncomfortable.

Work Environments That Allow HSPs to Thrive

Some highly sensitive people may enjoy working in the arts because, in general, they tend to be artistically talented. HSPs have a special connection to art because they have a fine appreciation of nuance and beauty. Their connection to creativity is often described as spiritual, since they have the ability to be deeply moved by a song or poem, and they see greater value in these things than most people. Additionally, working on art requires a great amount of solitude, which is perfect for HSPs. Creativity also has the power to make highly sensitive people feel seen, which is very important, especially when HSPs grew up feeling neglected or overlooked. The act of sharing a work of art with the world and receiving recognition from that art can have a profoundly healing effect on HSPs. It teaches them that they can express themselves loudly and proudly. Many HSPs long for attention and a sense that their special qualities are appreciated. Art is a worthwhile pursuit for highly sensitive people, so long as they don't get disappointed by inevitable rejections and setbacks.

Life as an artist can also be challenging because it puts the HSP in a vulnerable position. On the one hand, they are deeply intuitive, so creativity comes naturally to them; many HSPs are inherently gifted creatives, and the act of showing off their skills can prove deeply rewarding. But life as a creative person is also fraught with judgment and competition, and more often than not, it involves activities that don't come naturally to HSPs, such as networking and advertising. Nevertheless, art is a better fit than most career options for HSPs. It involves self-expression, solitude, depth, and reflection—all things HSPs crave and need. If you're an HSP with a specific artistic talent, don't be afraid to pursue it as a career. It could provide a deeply satisfying life full of purpose and meaning.

Another common vocation for highly sensitive people is anything in a helping profession. Needless to say,

HSPs understand emotions better than anyone else. They naturally know how to care for people in need. For this reason, many HSPs pursue careers as therapists, counselors, healers, or social workers. Careers such as these embrace HSP's natural skillset. Plus, highly sensitive people love to feel needed and appreciated for their emotional strength. Teaching is a worthwhile profession for the same reason. Anything that allows highly sensitive individuals to connect with and help others should prove deeply rewarding. Naturally, the same goes for animals too. Many HSPs feel a special connection to animals because they're vulnerable and often rely on the help of caring humans. They give love effortlessly, without the awkwardness that sometimes comes with human expressions of love. Therefore, working with animals is another way that HSPs can feel fulfilled through their work.

No matter what you choose to pursue as a highly sensitive person, it's important that your sensitivities are celebrated rather than taken advantage of. It's also essential that whatever you choose to do gives your life meaning and purpose. You should feel intrinsically motivated to do a good job so that you feel like you're making a valuable contribution to the larger world. HSPs feel the pain of the collective more profoundly than the average person. If they're doing a meaningless or trivial job while there are billions of people suffering around the world, HSPs will certainly grow depressed. They need something to motivate them, and more often than not, it's a quest for healing or profundity that sets their souls on fire.

Whatever it is that HSPs decide to pursue, they must recognize that they have a gift that deserves expression. It's easy for HSPs to get stuck in jobs where their unique skills aren't given value, their personalities aren't respected, and their needs aren't taken seriously. In these types of positions, HSPs can get caught in a cycle of people-pleasing or overcompensating, just to end up feeling exhausted and underappreciated. This is exactly the type of scenario HSPs should avoid at all costs. If you're an HSP who has had trouble finding a job or career you love, know your worth and don't settle for anything that makes you feel crummy. Life is too short to spend your days miserable. Listen to your intuition and go after whatever it is that makes your heart sing.

Chapter Summary

- Finding your true purpose takes time, so it's okay to try many different things before you settle into one specific career.

- Most highly sensitive people prefer jobs where they can work from home or work with people in a one-on-one capacity. Small talk can be incredibly draining for HSPs, so they should avoid jobs that place them in the throes of superficial conversation.

- Some highly sensitive people may enjoy working in the arts because in general, they tend to be artistically talented. Although life as an artist is also competitive and vulnerable, HSPs must assess the pros and cons of such a career.

- Many HSPs pursue careers as therapists, counselors, healers, or social workers. Careers such as these embrace HSP's natural skillset. Plus, highly sensitive people love to feel needed and appreciated for their emotional strength.

In the next chapter, you will learn about the unique impact of social media on highly sensitive people and how to detox when necessary.

CHAPTER EIGHT

The Impact of Social Media and How to Detox

"Even a moderate and familiar stimulation like a day at work can cause a highly sensitive person to need quiet by evening."
—Elaine N. Aron, psychologist and author

Social media is still a new phenomenon, but a phenomenon it is, nonetheless. It's become such a massive part of life that for most people, it's hard to escape. It's how we connect, network, and stay up to date on news and pop culture. It's also a means for self-expression, and in many ways, it's an excellent platform for highly sensitive people to put themselves out there without the anxieties that come with meeting new people at a party, for example. Nevertheless, social media can be overwhelming. Just its interface alone breeds overstimulation. It encourages comparison and opens the doors for unsolicited judgment. For these reasons, the impact of social media is a worthwhile topic to explore, especially when it comes to highly sensitive users.

Social Media's Negative Effects

For people both highly sensitive and not, social media can be overwhelming. At any given second, there's a flurry of new photos, updates, statuses, and news to catch up on. If you wanted to, you could scroll through platforms like Instagram and TikTok for hours on end, and many people do. In the midst of scrolling and exploring the apps, notifications pop up, messages from friends or acquaintances arrive, and upsetting images or videos are always around the corner. Obviously, this is a lot of stimulation for highly sensitive consumers. It can be incredibly overwhelming for a timid HSP to check social media, only to be approached by a flurry of acquaintances who see that they are "active" on the app. Many highly sensitive people would prefer to check up on people without the risk of engaging in conversation. This is just one example of how social media breeds overstimulation.

Even if you use platforms like Instagram or Facebook without the anxiety that often comes from random messages, the images and statuses themselves can be a source of overstimulation. As it is, HSPs need their fair share of solitude to rest and decompress from the chaos of life and other people. And since social media is like a digital representation of that chaos, it can be equally overwhelming. More often than not, HSPs will see statuses, comments, or images that trigger their emotions because they simply can't help it. When people go online to express their feelings, it has a profound effect on deeply-feeling people. There's no escaping it. And if you're an HSP who posts a lot of content and comments yourself, you may become overwhelmed by the nuances in feedback. If a friend doesn't like one of your photos, you may fixate on it. Or if someone comments something with a negative tone, you may internalize that poor reception. Of course, this isn't true for every HSP, but there's no doubt that social media has the power to be incredibly overwhelming.

The potential for overstimulation is just one factor to consider in the relationship between HSPs and social media. There's also the propensity for comparison to consider. When everyone is advertising themselves on one platform for the world to see, it's all too easy to compare yourself against the accomplishments or appearances of your peers. Comparison is a dangerous game for highly sensitive people. HSPs already have a tendency to compare themselves against others because they feel so different from the majority of the people out in the world. But comparison is always a negative and damaging experience. The only person we can truly compare ourselves against is ourselves. Every human is uniquely special and different, so comparison is a toxic activity with zero gain or rewards. Unfortunately, though, social media is a giant comparison platform. HSPs should realize that just because someone appears more accomplished than you, it doesn't mean they actually are. Everyone has their own secrets, hardships, and insecurities. Don't take what you see on social media at face value. Generally, people try to boost themselves up on social media; therefore, it can be an inaccurate portrayal of reality and a lousy means for assessing success.

Social media also opens the door for judgment in all shapes and sizes. Judgment plays a massive role in social media. Any time you're looking at an image, status, or comment someone has posted, you're judging it. That doesn't always mean that the judgments are negative, but they're still judgments nonetheless. Unfortunately, people feel that they have the freedom to be more antagonistic online than in real life due to the detached nature of social media. But highly sensitive people can't detach, even in the context of online communication. So you see how social media can be a terribly negative place for HSPs. Highly sensitive people are already prone to internalizing judgments more than the average person. So when they enter a space where judgments like that are inevitable, it can have disastrous results.

It is well advised when dealing with social media, or any judgment in general, to depersonalize the judgmental statements. More likely than not, the judgments are a reflection of insecurities or feelings within the person who is judging. They should not be internalized as truth. Instead, statements like this should be acknowledged as a subjective and deeply biased opinion. Social media is an epic mecca for judgment in all forms. If you do choose to partake in it, do so with awareness. Highly sensitive people feel judged, even under circumstances where judgment isn't aimed at them. It has to do with HSP's ability to pick up on subtle cues and nuances. They have a habit of subconsciously looking for judgments where there aren't any because some HSPs struggle with self-esteem and can't help but absorb everything. If you're an HSP who enjoys social media, make sure you protect yourself from judgmental overload. Don't fixate on comments or overthink nuances in your interactions. Social media doesn't have to be overstimulating if you know how to protect yourself from the negatives.

One of the greatest negatives to social media that has only grown more rampant with time is the constant exposure to unrealistic expectations. This is especially relevant today, as social media has grown in popularity. People and celebrities alike edit their pictures or advertise themselves with tons of makeup and plastic surgery. These people may appear beautiful or even close to "perfect," but it's all an artificial illusion in reality. Obviously, if you're an HSP who spends lots of time on Instagram, you're going to feel the inclination to judge your own appearance against these unrealistic images. That can be a highly overwhelming experience. Highly sensitive people should practice awareness when using social media. They should remind themselves that much of what they see is artificial, and it should not form a basis for any kind of comparison or self-assessment.

Social media platforms such as Instagram also have the capacity to breed a fear of rejection. This is especially true for younger users. You see images of your friends or acquaintances doing fun things and you wonder, "Why wasn't I invited?" Your mind can easily spiral into thoughts like, "Maybe they don't like me. Maybe I'm not cool enough." These thoughts are damaging to highly sensitive people who already have a tendency toward feeling misunderstood. The highly sensitive brain is already prone to overthinking and intuiting things that aren't necessarily true. If you're an HSP, you've probably experienced this a lot throughout your life.

Your mind gets fixated on a certain issue and plays out all the scenarios, nuances, and possibilities. Social media only provides a fraction of a person's reality, so it's easy to fill in the blanks and go down a rabbit hole. To avoid this, it's best to detach and get some space. Remember that the world is a much bigger place than social media would like us to believe. The only person who can truly make you feel rejected is yourself.

Additionally, social media can be addicting, whether you're an HSP or not. It's easy to spend hours upon hours on the various platforms, scrolling endlessly until you've forgotten why you even opened the app in the first place. Plus, highly sensitive people often have a tendency toward escapism, and some could be described as having obsessive personalities. For this reason, HSPs should check in with themselves and make sure that their harmless affinity toward social media doesn't transform into an all-encompassing addiction. Of course, it's fine to spend a chunk of your day on the internet, checking in with loved ones and exploring the latest news. But if your relationship with social media looks similar to a codependent relationship, then you should probably take measures to spend less time on the internet. Highly sensitive people have to look out for their mental health more than most individuals, and forming healthy habits is an essential part of that.

The Social Media Detox

Many people take social media breaks nowadays because social media can be such a source of overstimulation and toxicity. This may look different for everyone, but some form of detoxing may be necessary for HSPs who already have a low threshold for stimulation. If you're an HSP who often feels overwhelmed by social media, consider taking a break. You can delete the apps from your phone, if even temporarily. Or you could consider setting a timer on your apps if your phone allows it. That way, you can receive a notification when you've spent more than a certain number of hours or minutes on social media. You may also consider deleting your profile, or you can just skip checking it for a significant amount of time. Don't be afraid to detox if social media becomes too much to handle. Notice the way you respond when you're engaging with it, listen to the signals from your body, and take appropriate breaks when necessary.

It is not uncommon for highly sensitive people to experience physical symptoms when browsing through social media. In the same way that an HSP can't help but get teary-eyed or nervous when watching a gruesome animal documentary, apps like Instagram can trigger a wide variety of physical responses. It can manifest in a rapid heart rate, increase in sweat, nausea, headaches, etc. It's like anything else that puts the HSP at risk for overstimulation. Think about it: the news tends to be too stimulating for sensitive people already, and social media combines the news with a range of other updates and images. When you consider the notifications aspect of it all, with all the pings and random loud noises, it's no wonder social media can be overstimulating. It's like the most crowded shopping mall in the world, only it's on your phone, begging you to click it whenever you have a moment of downtime. So if you're an HSP, and social media is all too much for you, don't feel ashamed. It's a lot of stimulation on a tiny interface.

It's true that not every highly sensitive person will experience overstimulation on social media. Some may never experience it. Some may only experience it half of the time or a quarter of the time, but if you do find it overstimulating, understand that HSPs have a tendency to ruminate on bad feelings. Many HSPs claim that the unhappiness they experience while on social media lingers long past their exposure to it. For example, you could spend your morning scrolling through Instagram, see something triggering, and then go to work. But while you're at work, you can't stop your brain from thinking about the triggering thing. Or maybe you are able to distract yourself, but your body still experiences anxiety or other symptoms of stress. These are important things to consider when you decide to engage with social media. Be honest with yourself, and notice how your body reacts to it, not only while using social media but also afterward.

Many highly sensitive people choose not to engage with social media, simply because it doesn't do much for them. It's also common for HSPs to take a momentary detox, only to realize they're happier without it. There are many reasons for this, but one of the main reasons has to do with the artificial nature of social media. In general, social media lacks depth, which is an HSP's favorite thing in the world. Highly sensitive people are inherently deep people due to their natural depth of feeling. They typically hate small talk and anything surface or shallow. While social media does present opportunities for spirited debate or exploration of niche topics, it's overall very superficial. This may be another reason why highly sensitive people sometimes feel out of place on Instagram and other platforms. Introverted HSPs, in particular, may feel inauthentic when posting statuses, comments, or images. They prefer deep connections rooted in authenticity, and social media is more geared toward brief exchanges on shallow topics. This is the HSP's gift—their ability to see below the surface and find beauty in all that is deep and meaningful. Social media can make them feel insecure because it is a popular platform where everyone gathers to talk about appearances and celebrities. Therefore, social media has the potential to elicit the same sensation that an introverted HSP may experience at a bad party. It's a feeling of isolation and a sense of being misunderstood. If you're an HSP who often feels this way while spending time on social media, consider disengaging.

Cultivating Emotional Resilience

According to Preston Ni, a professor and private coach, "for many highly sensitive people, the key to managing oversensitivity is to utilize emotional immunity and sensory immunity strategies, to smartly calm and alleviate overstimulation" (Ni, 2018). Emotional immunity describes our ability to access emotional resilience. Just like physical immunity, we all have the ability to bounce back or even fend off unpleasant emotions with healthy awareness. This is a necessary skill to develop if you find social media overstimulating but still want to use it for its positive benefits.

Forbes released an article in 2018 on the power of emotional resilience and sensory immunity. It states, "Mental immunity is what happens when we condition our minds to not only expect fearful thoughts or external challenges, but to tolerate them when they arise.

It is shifting one's objective in life from avoiding pain to building meaning, recognizing that pain will be some part of the journey regardless." Mental and emotional immunity should not be confused with repressing emotions. Repressing emotions only leads to a stacking of pent-up anxiety until those feelings come bursting out one day. This is not a healthy way to handle emotions. Cultivating emotional immunity allows you to acknowledge your feelings, even the painful or negative ones, and discover meaning through accepting them. This way, you can go forward with the knowledge that every emotion has its lesson or purpose. You can apply this to the often overstimulating experience of social media, but also to any experience that is overstimulating to HSPs. Through cultivating emotional resilience, highly sensitive people can accept their emotions in any given situation, and they can proceed through life with more confidence and less fear (Wiest, 2018).

There are, of course, many positives and benefits to social media. It can be a brilliant way to express yourself, feel seen, and stay updated. It can also provide an excellent space to connect with others over shared interests. If you're a highly sensitive artist, as many HSPs are, it can provide an opportunity for networking and a vehicle through which you can showcase your art. As an HSP, you are responsible for checking in with yourself and making sure that your relationship with social media is a positive one. Try this exercise for guidance on how to navigate your relationship with social media:

1. Meditate on your experience interacting with social media. Imagine yourself using it and feel what that feels like in your body.

2. After about 5-10 minutes of focused mediation, notice how your body feels. Does it feel calm? Does it feel tense? If it doesn't feel good, that's a sign that you should consider altering your relationship with social media. Maybe consider taking a break if necessary.

More than anything else, HSPs must protect their sensitivities, and this should extend beyond creating boundaries with people. Platforms such as social media require boundaries as well. As long as you're being honest with yourself, and accepting your feelings when they arrive, you can enjoy all of the benefits that come from our highly social digital age.

Chapter Summary

- Social media can be overstimulating for highly sensitive people for a number of reasons. It has the propensity to negatively affect HSPs far more than the average person.

- Social media often encourages comparison, judgment, unrealistic expectations, and fear of missing out, each of which is harmful for HSPs.

- Social media has the potential to elicit the same sensation that an introverted HSP may experience at a bad party. It's a feeling of isolation and a sense of being misunderstood. If you're an HSP who often feels this way while spending time on social media, consider disengaging.

- For many highly sensitive people, the best method for managing overstimulation is to utilize emotional and sensory immunity strategies to stabilize overstimulation (Ni, 2018).

In the next chapter, you will learn how to effectively communicate with non-HSPs as a highly sensitive person.

CHAPTER NINE

How to Communicate with a Non-HSP as a Highly Sensitive Person

"As a highly sensitive person, I can sense your mood from a mile away. Don't try to hide it. You're not fooling me."
—Tracy M. Kusmierz, Communications Manager at Not for Profit Organization

For highly sensitive people, communication already presents its fair share of challenges. Many HSPs did not grow up in homes where their needs were given voice. Many were never encouraged to speak up, and furthermore, the majority of HSPs are also introverts.

When you have an introverted personality who grew up in a toxic environment, *and* they're easily overstimulated, you get a person who would rather withdraw than act as a source of conflict. For HSPs, communication can be a tricky issue. It's even more tricky if the person the HSP is trying to communicate with lacks sensitivity. How can HSPs communicate effectively with non-HSPs? What can they do to feel more confident in communication in general?

Gaining Courage to Face Confrontation

First and foremost, highly sensitive people must realize that shying away from communication always leads to more conflict in the end. The more HSPs bury their feelings, the more they let animosity and resentment build up. It's unhealthy for both the HSP and the people close to them. However, this is easier said than done. Highly sensitive people are so worried about the feelings of others and so uncomfortable with conflict that they'll often go to great lengths to avoid it—even when they

141

know that confrontation is in the best interest of everyone involved. Confrontation produces a wide variety of physical symptoms, and sometimes epic levels of anxiety for HSPs. Ultimately, this is one of HSP's greatest challenges in life. They have to muster enough courage and strength to confront issues head-on if they ever wish to have harmonious relationships. And there's nothing HSPs crave more than quality, fulfilling relationships. Instead of avoiding conflict, HPSs need to accept that confrontation is a necessary evil in any relationship. The sooner they accept this, the sooner they will be able to thrive and enjoy the deep connections they long for.

So how do HSPs gain enough courage to confront issues head-on? Therapy is a great resource for identifying the various blocks that keep HSPs from experiencing the level of intimacy they crave. Through therapy, highly sensitive people can explore their childhood triggers in a non-judgmental setting. They can use the therapeutic relationship as a model for how they experience other relationships. In this way, they can gain awareness and understanding. They can come to terms with their childhood baggage and see that whatever the source of their fears are, they probably serve no purpose in the HSP's adult life. Typically, it's a chaotic early home environment that leads to HSP's deep fear of conflict. If they grew up in a home where conflict meant toxic abuse, then they'll be deeply afraid of conflict as adults. Nature often colludes with nurture in this way. Highly sensitive people are predisposed to conflict-aversion because they're natural peacemakers and harmony seekers. They're also natural empaths, finding it easy to forgive and extend understanding to every type of person. At the same time, many highly sensitive people often experience hardship in childhood. Many grew up in abusive homes or with narcissistic parents or relatives. This creates a trauma response in which the highly sensitive individual would rather "die" than risk re-experiencing abuse. So you see why confrontation is a complicated matter for highly sensitive people. It not only goes against their very nature, but it also transports them to the heart of early childhood traumas.

Luckily, with awareness, understanding, and the help of a good therapist, HSPs can come to terms with this and learn how to confront people without risking immense anxiety. They can explain their sensitivities to the non-HSPs in their lives, and practice confronting things in small ways. It's impossible for highly sensitive people to become expert communicators overnight, and they shouldn't put that kind of pressure on themselves. But with acceptance and understanding, they can take small measures to feel more comfortable with conflict.

The only way to accomplish this is through baby steps. HSPs can start by setting small boundaries with friends. They can practice confrontation with low stakes at first, so that they don't put too much pressure on themselves. For example, a highly sensitive person may have trouble telling their friend that something they said or did hurt their feelings. But with a therapist, they have a safe container in which to express their needs. If a therapist disappoints a highly sensitive person by missing an appointment or saying something that was accidentally hurtful, the HSP has an opportunity to confront the therapist without risking any negative consequences. That way, HSPs can get used to confrontation in an objectively safe space. Then, they can learn that confrontation doesn't always end badly, and they can feel more confident when confronting people in their everyday lives.

If confronting your therapist is still too frightening, you can opt for even lower-stakes opportunities. Practice confronting a telemarketer or someone in a service position. Obviously, this doesn't mean you should harass your server at the Cheesecake Factory, but if you're in a situation where your feelings are triggered, where you feel that you've been treated unfairly or have been disrespected, don't be afraid to address it. Confrontation doesn't mean being aggressive. You can address your feelings with someone while also being polite and working toward a more productive relationship. There are opportunities for this all the time, in every shape and form. It's the HSP's job to look for them and act upon them. The more highly sensitive people practice confrontation in low-stakes situations, the better prepared they'll be when confronting matters in serious relationships. Again, confrontation is a necessary evil. HSPs have the right to have their feelings heard and their needs met.

Understanding Common Triggers

Besides confrontation, there are a few other common fears HSPs experience that can manifest as major obstacles when communicating with non-HSPs. For instance, some highly sensitive people experience fight-or-flight reactions to emotional triggers. Generally, the main sources of these reactions are self-doubt, self-criticism, self-judgment, fear of upsetting people, and negative self talk. If someone puts an HSP in a situation that brings up a lot of self-doubt, they may react with bursts of emotions that appear irrational to non-HSPs. However, these reactions are perfectly natural, especially when you consider how the majority of HSPs were raised. So let's explore each of these issues more thoroughly. That way, if you're an HSP yourself, you can understand why you react so strongly to seemingly insignificant encounters.

Self-doubt is a major trigger for highly sensitive people. HSPs tend to doubt themselves far more than the average person, partly due to their nuanced lens, and partly due to their fluctuating self-esteem. There's also something to be said of HSP's heightened relationship with empathy. When it's easy to put yourself in another person's shoes, it's also easy to undervalue or confuse your own experience. You may think, "Well, I thought I felt this way about this situation, but if they're saying they feel differently, maybe I should adjust my thinking." However, these kinds of thoughts can prove dangerous. Highly sensitive people are also highly emotionally intelligent. They have strong intuitions and their greatest strength lies in their ability to accurately judge every kind of human interaction. The self-doubt that is so common to HSPs is usually a product of overthinking. It's not actually rooted in any real inferiority. Although HSPs often feel inferior, their gifts of intuitive insight make them better equipped to assess interactions than most people. If you're an HSP who often doubts yourself when dealing with other people, don't second guess. Trust your heightened intuition and trust that you do have an accurate lens.

Equally, HSPs have difficulties with self-criticism and negative self-talk in general. Of course, this presents challenges when it comes to relating closely with others. It's easiest to bond with other people when we feel good about ourselves deep inside. If you don't feel good about yourself, you'll exude an energy that says, "I'm not warm" or "I don't have anything to offer others." Of course, this couldn't be further from the truth, but these kinds of negative sentiments are common internal statements for highly sensitive people. HSPs tend to be overly forgiving of others and overly critical of themselves. Not only does this prevent HSPs from experiencing the closeness they crave, but it also creates a kind of sickness of the mind. When we talk negatively to ourselves, we're telling ourselves that we're not worthy, that we can't meet our own expectations. If you do this enough, you can experience negative physical symptoms and high levels of depression and anxiety. Be kind to yourself. Treat yourself the way you would treat a close friend. Don't be so hard on yourself. Every human being is perfect, exactly as they are. The sooner HSPs realize this, the sooner they can live free and happy lives.

We already discussed how HSPs value authenticity above all else. They hate small talk and artificiality in all forms. But this doesn't necessarily mean that authentic self-expression comes naturally to every highly sensitive person. Many struggle to speak authentically, even though the alternative means being fake. Still, because HSPs have such a strong desire to please and relate, they often express themselves less authentically than they'd like to. For example, if a new friend has a strong opinion about something, and the HSP has the opposite opinion, the HSP may tip-toe around the issue. They may avoid stating their true opinion on the subject because they're worried about upsetting the other person, or worse, causing conflict. But this presents a challenge for highly sensitive people because deep bonds are born out of authenticity. If you're an HSP who finds yourself sugar-coating your strong opinions or faking certain interactions in order to maintain harmony, try a different approach instead. Try committing yourself to honesty and living everyday like the most authentic version of yourself possible. Just like confrontation, this is one of those areas of life that proves especially challenging for highly sensitive people. But the best way to overcome it is just through the art of practice. If you commit yourself to living by your truth, in small ways at first, you'll eventually wonder why you spent so much time masking your feelings for the sake of harmony.

All the struggles we've covered in this chapter so far are responses to anxiety. Typically, they're not the kind of responses that garner a lot of thought. They tend to be fight-or-flight reactions, immediate and spontaneous. That doesn't mean that HSPs won't fixate on them later, but they often occur with little time for the HSP to think or decide on a course of action. If you're an HSP, it may be helpful to notice these fight-or-flight symptoms when they arrive so that you can put more thought into your response. For highly sensitive people, awareness is everything. It can mean the difference between expressing yourself authentically and saying something you didn't mean, only to beat yourself up about it later. If HSPs can notice the symptoms in their bodies as they occur, they can operate from a place of knowing and confident self-awareness. These symptoms include memory loss, getting flushed, sweating, or rapid heart rate. If you're in a situation where you feel like you suddenly can't remember something, take a deep breath and understand that this is just a result of overstimulation. Then, instead of reacting on impulse, you can think about how you'd like to respond before you do so.

Another typical trigger for HSP's fight-or-flight response comes in the form of dominant people. Highly sensitive types tend to attract dominant personalities like a magnet. On the one hand, this is beneficial to HSPs, since HSPs tend to be more timid and less assertive; highly sensitive people could use a good push every now and then, and dominant personalities are there to give it. On the other hand, it's easy for HSPs to feel bulldozed or taken advantage of in these situations. When hanging out with someone who is demanding or talkative, highly sensitive people can feel easily overwhelmed. This is why boundaries are important. Again, if you're an HSP who has dominant people in your life, notice how your body responds when interacting with them. Take a breath and a break if necessary. Always choose honesty over avoidance.

Highly sensitive people often face a lot of turmoil at work, where they have to interact with many non-HSPs in stressful situations. Here, too, HSPs are likely to run into many dominant personalities. It can be difficult for highly sensitive people to speak up at work or make sure their thoughts are heard. It's even more difficult if they're the only HSP in the office. HSPs may have many brilliant ideas about how to make the company more money or how to create a more peaceful and productive work environment, but if they feel that they can't speak up, those ideas get repressed, and they end up feeling inadequate or undervalued. Highly sensitive people should do what they can to avoid this. They can speak with their superiors or a trusted coworker in a private setting. They can also try communicating their ideas in written form, through digital correspondence. This way, they can process their thoughts more thoroughly before speaking, and they can communicate without the pressure that comes from spontaneous verbal exchange. Highly sensitive people deserve to feel safe while expressing their thoughts and ideas. If those around them aren't able to provide that safety, HSPs must do what they can to establish it themselves.

Outside of work, HSPs have other communication quirks that may seem odd to non-HSPs. For example, many highly sensitive people have bizarre relationships with their phones. Cell phones are a source of overstimulation for many highly sensitive people. Sometimes they have a backlog of text messages they have yet to respond to. The same goes for emails and social media notifications. Sometimes HSPs will leave their phone somewhere on purpose just to avoid the stress that comes with too much social stimulation. This isn't true for every HSP, of course, but it's common nonetheless. If you're a highly sensitive person who easily feels overwhelmed by the demands of your cell phone, don't be afraid to take breaks from it, and don't listen to people who demand you spend more time answering texts. Everyone deserves a break now and then, especially highly sensitive folks.

Non-HSPs should also try to understand the highly sensitive person's relationship with resentment. Resentment is usually a result of an unbalanced partnership. There are many reasons why HSPs tend to be overly giving in their relationships. Sometimes, they feel that it's what they have to do in order to maintain harmony. Other times, it's due to a general sense of inadequacy or low self-esteem. Either way, highly sensitive people are also highly empathetic, and they want to go the extra mile for the people in their lives. However, if they start to feel like they're giving more than they're receiving, resentment will certainly build up. To avoid this kind of situation, HSPs should only give as much as they receive. They should never overcompensate or sacrifice their own needs for the sake of someone else.

Highly sensitive people have needs just like everyone else, but more often than not, HSPs would prefer to skate through life without ever addressing their needs out of fear of feeling like a burden. This is a paradox because HSPs rarely see the needs of others as burdensome. While they jump through hoops trying to meet everyone else's needs, there's no one there to make sure the HSP's needs are being met. Obviously, this is unfair, but it's the HSP's responsibility to make sure that their needs are being accounted for. With time, patience, and practice, highly sensitive people can learn to express their needs and desires with greater ease. This is especially important during moments of confrontation. Generally, highly sensitive people are overcompromising in the face of conflict. With all the pressure and overstimulation, they'd rather give in and even appear wishy-washy than state their needs concretely. This, too, can lead to resentment and turmoil in close relationships.

Communication is a tricky issue for highly sensitive people, and it's made even more tricky when it involves a non-highly sensitive person. Often, people need a little help understanding one another. It's true for everyone, sensitive or not. Everyone is made differently, and everyone could benefit from a little more understanding. HSPs should give their non-HSP loved ones the opportunity to understand them, whether it's showing them this book, sending a video link, or explaining their experience. With understanding, we have the opportunity to grow together, learn from one another, and gain more insight into the human experience. We can inspire others through the power of empathy, and teach the whole human race to celebrate each other's differences. It all starts with communication and openness. Highly sensitive people have a special gift to offer loved ones, and the greater world as a whole. If you're a highly sensitive person, offer your gift freely. Spread the abundant love and warmth you feel inside, and shine brightly with passion and gratitude.

Chapter Summary

- Highly sensitive people must realize that shying away from communication always leads to more conflict in the end. The more HSPs bury their feelings, the more they let animosity and resentment build up.

- Therapy is a great resource for identifying the various blocks that keep HSPs from experiencing the level of intimacy they crave. They can use the therapeutic relationship as a model for how they experience other relationships. In this way, they can gain awareness and understanding.

- Some highly sensitive people experience fight-or-flight reactions to emotional triggers. Generally, the main sources of these reactions are self-doubt, self-criticism, self-judgment, fear of upsetting people, and negative self-talk.

- HSPs should give their non-HSP loved ones the opportunity to understand them, whether it's showing them this book, sending a video link, or explaining their experience—as difficult as that can be for highly sensitive types.

In the next chapter, you will learn how to understand highly sensitive people if you're a non-highly sensitive person.

CHAPTER TEN

Understanding HSP from a
Non-HSP Perspective

"You cannot make everyone think and feel as deeply as you do. This is your tragedy, because you understand them but they do not understand you"
—Daniel Saint, poet and author

Life as a highly sensitive person can feel lonely and isolating at times. When you make up a rare percentage of the population, it's easy to feel misunderstood. Since HSPs absorb 80 percent more stimuli than the average person, they can literally feel how others experience life differently from them. It's almost like highly sensitive people can tap into the emotions of others and experience firsthand how others feel less than them. You see, then, how this can be incredibly frustrating for the HSP. They understand the experiences of everyone else, yet only a small fraction of the population can fully understand the HSP's experience, at least on an emotional level. But this doesn't mean that HSPs are unable to form deep bonds with non-HSPs.

If you are **not** a highly sensitive person but have a highly sensitive loved one in your life, do what you can to make your HSP feel understood. Start by reading this chapter and reflecting on the various differences in your psychological makeup. There's a lot to be learned, and there's a lot to be gained through deep bonds with highly sensitive people. But those deep bonds can only manifest through mutual understanding and awareness.

Awareness and Education

There are several common misunderstandings that non-HSPs form about HSPs. This doesn't mean that every non-HSP lacks emotional intelligence or is incapable of understanding the HSP's emotional experience; it just means that there are certain assumptions people make because they lack sufficient knowledge. For example, some non-HSPs may look at a highly sensitive person and wonder, "Can't they just toughen up?" or "Why do these people take things so personally?" But HSPs know that it's not a matter of taking things personally, nor is it a matter of simply "toughening up." Highly sensitive people have hyper sensitive neurons. Their brains take in far more information than the average person, and this isn't something they have any control over. So if you're an HSP whose friend or acquaintance has the wrong idea about your sensitivities, understand that they may not have the facts right. In general, many people are unaware that there even is such a thing as highly sensitive people. Most people don't know that about 20 percent of the population has sensitive mirror neurons. It's easy to assume when you don't have all the facts. If you're a non-HSP, please don't insist that your HSP friend "toughen up." Instead, understand that their brain has certain genetic differences that make "toughening up" impossible. Use it as a learning moment, and hopefully everyone will have a better understanding of sensitivity in just a few years.

Additionally, non-HSPs may complain that they have to walk on eggshells around their highly sensitive friends or loved ones. They may assume that any little remark will surely set the HSP off, which can be incredibly disheartening for the highly sensitive individual. But the truth is, everyone is responsible for their own emotions, and most highly sensitive people are comfortable taking responsibility for their feelings. Plus, the majority of HSPs are also highly empathetic. They don't want to make anyone feel uncomfortable, and they'd hate to hear that their friend or loved one feels less than safe around them. Many HSPs have had to walk on eggshells throughout their childhoods due to a narcissistic parent or an abusive authority figure. Even more have dealt with toxic friendships or abusive romantic relationships in their adult lives. But these experiences give the HSP a great amount of emotional maturity and intelligence. More likely than not, if a friend of an HSP feels that they have to walk on eggshells around them, the HSP will pick up on that feeling and do whatever they can to alleviate their friend's stress.

If you're a non-HSP, understand that highly sensitive people often worry about making their friends or family uncomfortable. But through reading a little about highly sensitive people, you have all the tools necessary to create a harmonious and relaxing atmosphere. More likely than not, the HSPs in your life should inform you that they take full responsibility for their emotions, and they don't expect anything from you when they're feeling overstimulated. If they have to, they should find a private space where they can withdraw when they become too stimulated, a safe place just for them. Whatever you do, avoid making your HSP loved one feel like their sensitivity is a burden on them. It's that same sensitivity which makes them an easygoing friend who is warm and affectionate. No one should have to walk on eggshells, and no one comprehends that better than highly sensitive people.

The biggest misunderstanding that often occurs between highly sensitive people and non-HSPs comes up during conflict. First of all, conflict is one of the most overstimulating experiences an HSP can possibly encounter. For HSPs, the brain becomes so overstimulated during conflict that it nearly shuts down.

For example, if someone is yelling at an HSP, or even venting for hours on end, the HSP will have trouble keeping up. Part of this has to do with the way HSPs process information: they prefer to think deeply about things, so they can't just move on to the next topic before they've addressed the current one. This can be frustrating for people whose brains work much faster. They may wonder why their HSP loved one can't keep up, or worse, they may blame the HSP for not paying attention. However, it's not a matter of paying attention. It's a matter of depth of thought. HSPs can't help the way their brains process information, so as a non-HSP, you should try to create space in conversations for HSPs to process everything. That way, there's no room for misunderstanding.

There are certain tactics highly sensitive people can use to make sure that conflict is productive. One thing they can do is take a time out when things become too heated. This may seem counter-productive to the non-HSP, but it can mean the difference between an effective conversation and an utter impasse. If you have an HSP in your life who easily feels overwhelmed in the face of conflict, don't be afraid to give your HSP the time they need to process before continuing the conversation. Understand that they're very prone to overstimulation and that breaks help them focus and stay on track. They also help them absorb your words and feelings with more clarity. Hopefully, the HSP has enough courage to communicate these needs to you. Then, you can both have a healing conversation with necessary breaks if that's what's needed.

Strange HSP Habits

Besides the general overwhelm that HSPs often experience, there are some additional habits that non-highly sensitive types may have trouble understanding. Again, HSPs are a rare breed, making up only a fraction of the population. It's no wonder they have certain idiosyncrasies and habits that look far different from the average person. Still, HSPs should always avoid the temptation to mold themselves into something they're not. They should accept themselves exactly as they are, "strange" habits and all. It's always beneficial for HSPs to communicate with non-HSPs about their habits and needs. Everyone has the capacity to understand highly sensitive people on an intellectual level. So why not provide the opportunity and insight? If you're reading this as a non-HSP, why wouldn't you want all the information you can get?

We already discussed how highly sensitive people need time and space to think thoroughly about things. Because they process so many sensory details, they need to funnel those details before they can make sense of the full picture. This is just how their brains work. Also, HSPs are hyper-aware of life's nuances, which adds to the depth of information processing. They understand the importance of details, so they need ample time to reflect on them before drawing conclusions. This is why many HSPs carve out time for doing nothing but thinking. To non-HSPs, it may seem very bizarre. Highly sensitive people are often eager for a moment of solitude to reflect on all the energy they've absorbed and make room for new energy as well.

It can also be difficult for non-HSPs to understand that highly sensitive people often feel strong feelings over small events. A movie or sad song, for example, has the power to affect HSPs in a profound way. To non-HSPs, it may seem insignificant, but to someone who absorbs 80 percent more energy than the average person, it's quite natural. Plus, highly sensitive people tend to be more aware of their emotional state at any given moment. Even a slight ping of sadness has the potential to take up a large amount of space in an HSP's brain. On the other hand, a non-HSP may have the power to brush a small feeling under the rug. This leads to the next odd habit that highly sensitive people are known for:

Many HSPs require a great deal of time before they can make a proper decision on matters. To non-HSPs, this can feel frustrating. But again, it's all due to the deep feeling nature of HSPs. When you're prone to overstimulation the way highly sensitive people are, every decision, big or small, has greater risks. HSPs want to set themselves up to experience the least amount of anxiety and stress possible. So decision making can be difficult. But HSPs are also highly conscientious, which can be very valuable in relationships and in the context of life in general. Although it may frustrate non-HSPs, highly sensitive people have a lot to offer through their thorough thinking and cautious natures.

By the same token, many highly sensitive people also feel drained after performing common tasks. That's just part of the highly sensitive package. If you're a non-HSP, you may find it strange that your HSP needs time to decompress after going to the grocery store or shopping mall. Life inside a hyper-sensitive brain can be taxing, and HSPs have every right to a break every now and then. Sometimes, highly sensitive people need random naps or brief moments of solitude before they have the energy to take on life again. If you live with, or are close with an HSP who requires consistent down-time after various tasks throughout their day, allow them that time. If you have a problem with it, the HSP may one day realize that you are not a friend worth keeping.

With all that being said, it's no surprise that many HSPs also have a desire to leave social events early from time to time. Socializing can be exhausting, especially for highly sensitive people who are typically introverted. This doesn't mean that all HSPs hate parties or social gatherings, but highly sensitive people do detest small talk. Too much exposure to shallow conversation can leave highly sensitive people feeling immensely drained. If you're a non-HSP who is in a relationship with an HSP, let them explain their reasons for feeling overstimulated at social gatherings, and don't be afraid to let them leave events early if they have to. It doesn't mean the party has to stop for everyone.

As much of the previous information in this chapter suggests, highly sensitive people tend to be the "slow-burner" type. They take time to absorb all the details, they take time to process things, and they take time to make decisions. So HSPs generally need ample time to feel comfortable before jumping into anything new. This goes for relationships, new jobs, warming up to a new friend group, etc. So it's no surprise that this bleeds into their ability to connect with others as well. HSPs love deep connections more than anything in the world, but they aren't the ones to reveal everything all at once. Instead, they'd rather suss people out slowly. They need time to feel comfortable, especially if they're going to open themselves up and show vulnerability to a new person.

HSPs also have vivid inner worlds. They can try to spend less time in their heads through the practice of mindfulness and meditation. But they can't help that their inner worlds are always communicating subtle details to them. This is probably the most unusual quirk from a non-HSP's perspective. If you're not someone who has movies playing in your mind half the time, then it's quite difficult to relate. As a non-HSP friend or lover, you may assume that the HSP is not paying attention to you, when really, their brain is working on overdrive, making sense of deep thoughts. Furthermore, for HSPs, it's easy to get so caught up in their inner world that they miss obvious things in their environment. For example, they may miss a turn while driving because they just had a revelation about the meaning of life; it sounds silly, but this is not uncommon. To non-HSPs, it may read as unfocused. Non-HSPs should try to understand the HSP's experience for this reason. Their brains simply operate differently. Clarity can ward off many potential misunderstandings.

We already discussed how highly sensitive people loathe small talk and any situation that lacks depth, but it's important for non-HSPs to understand just how uncomfortable inauthentic social gatherings are for HSPs. Any situation or event that has a less than authentic social etiquette will make HSPs uncomfortable. They may feel out of place or insecure in such a setting because to participate feels like putting on an act. HSPs are deeply feeling people—they're not programmed to exist on the shallow plane of life. Non-HSPs should try their best to understand this and assist their HSPs when they feel uncomfortable due to inauthentic social etiquette.

And, of course, HSPs crave deep conversation. Typically, they're not very good at small talk because it's so foreign to their nature. This can make HSPs feel anxious in situations where they have to engage in it. But HSPs should learn to accept this part of themselves and either do what they can to turn shallow conversations into deeper ones or disengage when the small talk becomes overwhelming. As a non-HSP, you should try to understand this about the HSPs in your life so you can adequately help them in these situations. HSPs love to attend parties with a close confidant who can save them from shallow encounters. And, typically, non-

HSPs love to be that special person to an HSP. Don't be afraid to step in and be a good friend when attending social gatherings with highly sensitive people. That way, they always have someone to escape to a corner with. It provides a nice safety net for the deep-feeling HSP.

Highly sensitive people also have a greater concern for how their subtle interactions affect others. The slightest shift in energy during a conversation with a new person can send HSPs into a head spin. They want so badly to make others feel comfortable that any awkwardness in the slightest interaction can make HSPs feel guilty. This may seem odd to non-HSPs. Most people don't fixate on things like this. But non-HSPs must understand that this is simply part of the highly sensitive package. When you're hyper focused on energies and other people, it's easy to feel dejected or to blame yourself when conversations go south. HSPs should learn to ruminate less, and non-HSPs should help their HSP buddies to stay in the moment.

Highly sensitive people are also highly compassionate, and non-HSPs may be taken aback by how far their compassion extends. For example, when a fight

171

between two people breaks out, HSPs find it easy to feel empathy for both parties. This is even true for situations when one person is clearly in the wrong. To non-HSPs, it may feel ridiculous to feel bad for a bully. It may seem delusional or unproductive. But for highly sensitive individuals, it makes perfect sense. HSPs see more than the black and white interpretation of any given situation. They see everything in shades of gray. They understand that hurt people hurt people. It's not uncommon for highly sensitive people to show empathy and compassion for someone who is clearly in the wrong. This is part of their gift, and non-HSPs should try to understand this aspect of the HSP without judging it as delusional or misguided. The world can use more empathy.

Many of the traits that make highly sensitive people unique are grounded in overstimulation. HSPs are more easily stimulated than the average person. Naturally, this extends to sensory factors in the environment, such as bright lights, strong scents, or loud noises. Many HSPs feel overwhelmed in crowded places or in chaotic environments in general. They may experience a strong reaction to highly potent fragrances, and they may need to escape if the music is too loud at a party. When you consider the fact that HSPs have more sensitive mirror neurons, it's understandable that they'd feel overstimulated in chaotic situations. Any non-HSP who cares about their HSP loved one should understand and respect the HSP's high sensitivity to environmental factors.

Finally, non-HSPs should understand that highly sensitive people often shut down, and it's not always due to feeling depressed or angry. Once HSPs reach their threshold for overstimulation, they require a break. If circumstances don't allow them to take necessary breaks, their brains will shut down automatically. It's not because the highly sensitive individual is mean or stand-offish. It's just because their brains need time to reset after too much stimulation. HSPs should try to explain this to the non-HSPs in their lives in order to avoid misunderstanding. And non-HSPs should allow HSPs to be honest with them. Give them the space to explain, in detail, what's occurring if they're shutting down. If they're angry, don't be afraid to let them communicate that. But if they're simply overstimulated, give them the space to address that as well. Communication makes everything more clear.

It's a challenge for non-HSPs to fully grasp the highly sensitive experience. If you're not highly sensitive yourself, you don't have the same brain functions, which makes it impossible to understand the experience on an emotional level. Even so, anyone is capable of understanding on an intellectual level. And non-HSPs have much to gain from the companionship of highly sensitive people. HSPs can open non-HSP's minds, help them become more vulnerable and more spiritually enlightened. They have many gifts to offer people of every sensitivity level. If you're an HSP who often feels misunderstood by less sensitive types, understand that you have special qualities that benefit everyone you come into contact with. And if you're a non-HSP, let the HSPs in your life open your mind and your heart. I doubt you'll regret it.

Chapter Summary

- If you're a non-HSP, understand that highly

sensitive people often worry about making their friends or family uncomfortable. But through reading a little about highly sensitive people, you have all the tools necessary to create a harmonious and relaxing atmosphere.

- Many HSPs require a great deal of time before they can make a proper decision on matters. To non-HSPs, this can feel frustrating. But again, it's all due to the deep feeling nature of HSPs.

- Highly sensitive people need time and space to think thoroughly about things. Because they process so many sensory details, they need to funnel those details before they can make sense of the full picture.

- Any situation or event that has a less than authentic social etiquette will make HSPs extremely uncomfortable. They may feel out of place or insecure in such a setting because to participate feels like putting on an act.

Conclusion

Highly sensitive people have a rare gift. With the ability to intuit what other people are feeling, they have profound insight that most people don't have access to. Despite the challenges that come with their sponge-like quality, highly sensitive people have a special blessing. They can experience the world in a deeper, richer way, and they can use that experience and perspective to inspire others. Highly sensitive people have an inherent glow combined with a natural understanding of life around them. They can inspire others through art, direct support, casual conversation, or spiritual healing. The methods through which highly sensitive people choose to use their gifts are plentiful and diverse.

If you're a highly sensitive person yourself, embrace your sensitivities. Celebrate them and honor your unique gift. It is only through owning your specialness that you gain access to the abundance of power at your disposal. Highly sensitive people have a calling to restore empathy to the human collective. It's a big job, but highly sensitive people have even bigger hearts. Are you up for the task?

Thank You

Before you leave, I'd just like to say, thank you so much for purchasing my book.

I spent many days and nights working on this book so I could finally put this in your hands.

So, before you leave, I'd like to ask you a small favor.

Would you please consider posting a review on the platform? Your reviews are one of the best ways to support indie authors like me, and every review counts.

Your feedback will allow me to continue writing books just like this one, so let me know if you enjoyed it and why. I read every review and I would love to hear from you. To leave a review simply scan the QR code below or go to Amazon.com, go to "Your Orders" and then find it under "Digital Orders".

Scan a QR Code Below to Leave a Review:

Amazon US   Amazon Uk

Resources

Arabi, Shahida. (2020, July.) "The Highly Sensitive Person's Guide to Dealing with Toxic People: How to Reclaim Your Power From Narcissists and Other Manipulators." Accessed on 2/26/2022 https://www.amazon.com/Highly-Sensitive-Persons-Dealing-People/dp/1684035309/ref=asc_df_1684035309/?tag=hyprod-20&linkCode=df0&hvadid=509159807707&hvpos=&hvnetw=g&hvrand=7134101444972281304&hvpone=&hvptwo=&hvqmt=&hvdev=c&hvdvcmdl=&hvlocint=&hvlocphy=9031132&hvtargid=pla-939160468737&psc=1&asin=1684035309&revisionId=&format=4&depth=1

Aron, Elaine A. (2020, June). "The Highly Sensitive Person." Accessed on 3/5/2022 https://www.google.com/books/edition/The_Highly_Sensitive_Person/KZwhAgAAQBAJ?hl=en&gbpv=1&printsec=frontcover

Homberg, Judith. (2017, May 15). "High Sensitivity as a Vulnerability Factor in Substance Abuse." Accessed on 3/2/2022 https://www.zonmw.nl/en/news-and-funding/news/detail/item/high-sensitivity-as-a-vulnerability-factor-in-substance-abuse/

Ni, Preston. (2018, February 25). "10 Signs You're Highly Sensitive to Social Media." Accessed on 2/18/2022 https://www.psychologytoday.com/us/blog/communication-success/201802/10-signs-you-re-highly-sensitive-social-media

Philips, Lindsey. (2019, September 24). "Finding Strength in Sensitivity." Accessed on 2/20/2022 https://ct.counseling.org/2019/09/finding-strength-in-sensitivity/

Sensitive Evolution. (2012, September 9). "The DOES Model: Depth of Processing." Accessed on 2/20/2022 https://sensitiveevolution.com/sensitive-evolution-library/does-model-elaine-aron/does-model-depth-of-processing/

Torres, Felix. (2020, October). "What is Depression?" Accessed on 2/20/2022 https://www.psychiatry.org/patients-families/depression/what-is-depression

Wiest, Brianna. (2018, March 8). "7 Ways to Become More Mentally Immune and Emotionally Resilient." Accessed on 3/1/2022 https://www.forbes.com/sites/briannawiest/2018/03/08/

7-ways-to-become-more-mentally-immune-and-emotionally-resilient/?sh=48404b8b528a

Ward, Deborah. (2012, October 5). "Coping with Anxiety as an HSP." Accessed on 2/19/2022 https://www.psychologytoday.com/us/blog/sense-and-sensitivity/201210/coping-anxiety-hsp

Printed in Great Britain
by Amazon

86083996R00109